WHAT THEY ARE SAYING ABOUT
DEFENDER OF THE DUNES

It amazes me still to realize that Kathleen Goddard Jones actually STOPPED the nuclear power plant on property PG&E had already purchased on the dunes. . . I had assumed this book would be tedious reading—it wasn't—it was an interesting story of a person I had known only from one part of her life.

Bill Denneen, Dune activist

Cornell has caught the very spirit of the woman—her determination, her passionate devotion, her ability to inspire and educate. I hope the book will find its way into the hands of us faltering defenders of our private sacred spaces, to lend us her determination.

Judith Goodman, Nature activist and radio personality

The dialogue reads like Cornell was there taking notes!

Jack Beigle, Dune guide and naturalist

I was fascinated! I commend Cornell for writing this—because without writers like her looking into heroic stories like this, such inspirations might be lost.

Hillary Hauser, **Heal the Ocean**

DEFENDER
OF THE DUNES

The Kathleen Goddard Jones Story

Virginia Cornell

MANIFEST PUBLICATIONS

CARPINTERIA, CALIFORNIA

2 0 0 1

DEFENDER OF THE DUNES
The Kathleen Goddard Jones Story

by Virginia Cornell

Manifest Publications
P.O. Box 429
Carpinteria, CA 93014-0429 U.S.A.
www.manifestpub.com

Printed in the United States of America on recycled paper

Publishers Cataloging-in-Publication
Cornell, Virginia.
    Defender of the Dunes : the Kathleen Goddard Jones Story / Virginia Cornell.
        p. cm.
        ISBN: 1-929354-06-1

        LC Control Number
        2001 129125

Cover Photography:
Front Dunes courtesy of Photodisc; Lone Figure by Nicholas Dean
Rear Dunes & River by Nicholas Dean; Kathleen Goddard Jones by Betty Usher

Cover and Book Design by Valentina Laurence Pfeil

TABLE OF CONTENTS

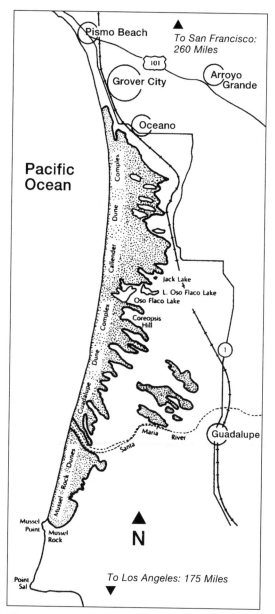

The Nipomo Dunes stretch eighteen miles, covering 18,000 acres, along the Central California Coast between Pismo Beach to the north and Vandenberg Air Force Base to the south. The nearest major cities are San Luis Obispo (18 miles) and Santa Barbara (75 miles) away.

AUTHOR'S NOTE

THE FIRST TIME I MET KATHLEEN GODDARD JONES she did a curious thing. I had been waiting for her in front of her house in Arroyo Grande, California. When she finally emerged from her battered Ford Pinto, the small energetic woman apologized profusely for being late from a luncheon appointment. Then she stuck the leather case attached to her car keys firmly between her teeth. The keys dangled as she rummaged through her purse in search of her house key.

Later, when I hiked with her onto the dunes the importance of that key-clenching maneuver became apparent when she taught me that if you absolutely must protect something from falling into the gritty sand, be it a camera, glove, or a plastic baggie with a sandwich in it, the surest way to secure it is to clamp it between your teeth. Even in small habits, Kathleen was never far from her beloved dunes.

The success of my first book, *Doc Susie: The True Story of a Country Physician in the Colorado Rockies*, taught me that readers harbor a hunger to learn more about the exploits of their foremothers. When I began looking around for another heroine, someone who had really accomplished something, I had difficulty finding just the right woman.

I decided to ask Henry Brown, a friend of my family. He grew up and lived much of his life in Carpinteria. Later he moved to Kern County where he wrote books about environmentalism.

"Henry," I said one day. "I'm looking for a woman who really *did something.*"

Without hesitation he replied, "Why, that would be Kathleen Goddard Jones."

"And what did she do?" I asked.

"She saved the Nipomo Dunes. I'll introduce you to her."

One blustery March day in 1995 Henry and I drove the two hours north to Arroyo Grande. On the way we stopped at Oso Flaco Lake, my introduction to the dunes. He led me through a cold, wintry rain across the lake's new footbridge and onto the adjacent dunes. In a few minutes we saw the ocean which was very angry that day; rollers attacked the shore with a vengeance. Although we didn't stay long I understood at once that the dunes were a place of drama and grandeur, a setting that demanded attention.

Kathleen agreed to talk to me while leading me onto the dunes. We spent several happy days marching about; more than once we got lost. She taught me about flowers, showed me the curious track of crickets, worked to transfer her gospel of conservation to me. I hauled along a little tape recorder, which played back Kathleen's commentary along with a lot of wind turbulence. I always hurried home to transcribe the tapes. As it turned out, I was probably the last person with whom Kathleen explored the dunes.

Unfortunately, my intention to write a book immediately got sidetracked. Kathleen was badly hurt in an accident on Thanksgiving Eve that year. Then I worked with two authors to publish six more books, and wrote one myself as well.

Fortunately, I was not the only person who had worked with Kathleen. Anne Van Tyne contacted Kathleen for the Sierra Club Oral History Project in 1983. Her interview was published with introductions by John Ashbaugh and Dirk Walters in 1984.

Kathleen's friend Judith Goodman from Big Sur recorded eleven tapes with Kathleen in 1992. Excellently catalogued, they have been a very great help. Judith hopes one day to use some of the material for radio presentations.

No story can be told from just one side. Ken Diercks, the representative Pacific Gas and Electric Company sent to San Luis Obispo County, has spoken with me on several occasions. His insights into Kathleen's dynamic character were very helpful.

Veteran outdoorsman Bill Denneen has been generous in many ways. He granted an interview, then said, "Here are my files, this drawer is labeled Kathleen, and there is my copier. Feel free to copy anything you want." His material was well organized and included valuable letters from Kathleen—letters written at the time of the controversy. I hiked with Bill Denneen and came to recognize that he has become an organic part of the dunes.

Jack Beigle and his wife Grace have served as unofficial guardian angels to Kathleen. Jack has generally been able to point me toward any information I needed. On one hike he gave a good explanation of the geologic history of the dunes.

Lela and Bernard Burdett provided an interesting perspective on a stormy period. Their quiet, behind-the-scene efforts helped Kathleen in ways she probably didn't even know about.

Henry Brown, and his daughter Emily Miles, gave me insights about Kathleen's trek into the Golden Trout Wilderness. Indirectly, it was Henry who sent me back to this project. When I learned that he was very ill and probably would not survive, I pledged to him on his deathbed that I would write this book. It's pretty hard to escape a promise like that.

Unfortunately, the archival material that Jack Beigle, Dominic Perello and I removed from Kathleen's back storeroom a few years ago remains unclassified in the Kennedy Library of California Polytechnic State University. When I contacted Dr. Nancy Loe in the Special Collections Department there did not appear to be any way to systematically examine its chaotic contents. The ultimate disposition of Kathleen's letters and accumulated papers remains in doubt. Therefore Lauren Roberts, my research assistant, and I spent several days in the periodicals room of the same library searching microfilm for news from the *San Luis Obispo Telegram-Tribune*.

Also helpful were Kathleen's daughter Gay Ferguson, Jim and Sue Higman, Harold Miossi, and Roberta Moran.

Liz Scott Graham, Dunes Program Manager, brought me up to date on the present situation of the dunes and showed me around the restored Craftsman house that the Dune Center now occupies in Guadalupe. Readers who would like to know more about the events surrounding this story are urged to consult my sources: Sierra Club Oral History Project, Kathleen Goddard Jones DEFENDER OF CALIFORNIA'S NIPOMO DUNES, STEADFAST SIERRA CLUB VOLUNTEER, 1984, interview by Anne Van Tyne; Michael P. Cohen, *The History of the Sierra Club 1892-1970*, Sierra Club Books, San Francisco, 1988; Marc J. Roberts and Jeremy S. Bluhm, *The Choices of Power: Utilities Face the Environmental Challenge*, Harvard University Press, Cambridge, Mass., 1981; Norm Hammond, *The Dunites*, South County Historical Society, 1992.

Patient proofreaders included Barbara Taylor, Blaine Patino, Lauren Roberts, Louise Upson, Frances Laurence, Faith Henkin, and Laura Smith. Without the help of my editor and friend, Ted Berkman, this book would have been dull indeed. He helped me sift through the chaff, locate the kernel of this story, then helped me to germinate, nurture and harvest Kathleen's extraordinary contribution into existence.

INTRODUCTION

PHOTOGRAPHED FROM A HUNDRED MILES out in space, California's Pacific shoreline is a sweeping curve of blue ocean and green-brown inland hills, broken halfway down by a slender ribbon of yellow. This sudden sliver of gold, eighteen miles long, is central California's sand dunes: variously labeled Pismo, Oceano, Callender, Guadalupe, or Mussel Rock but most often called the Nipomo Dunes. Nipomo is a Native American term meaning foot of the mountain.

Geologically, the dunes are new kids on the block. Some 20,000 years ago, although glaciers covered much of the North American continent, California's rugged mountains stopped them short. In that Pleistocene age, abundant rain nurtured lush plant life. One blustery day a downpour in the mid-state Santa Lucia Mountains ripped away the heavy roots which had been serving as secure platforms for rocks. One basketball-sized boulder, thus dislodged, slid down a hillside and splashed into a creek, where a bigger rock soon cracked it in two. Its sections rolled along the cascading creek, gradually being reduced by collisions and rotation to small stones, then to pebbles. Ultimately, in countless cases, the stones were ground to grains of light silica sand, trillions of which were swept down to a wide alluvial plain.

At the end of the Wisconsin Ice Age some 12,000 years ago the ocean was 200 feet below its present level; as the ocean rose, grains of sand were swept back into the broad curve of San Luis Bay.

Churned toward the shore, the sediment advanced with the current toward the shoreline. Repeatedly grains of sand were lifted, then fell or were dashed back to the sea bottom. After countless somersaults they were cast on shore.

One sunny day the sand dried out, transitioned to the mercy of another force of nature: wind. Grains were lifted in a wave-like movement up and over a seashell on the beach where they dropped behind it in a formation called a sand shadow. A wind of only eleven miles an hour is sufficient to scuttle individual grains. When sand blew over a larger obstruction, perhaps a piece of driftwood or a plant, tall foredunes were formed along the beach to be stabilized by native plants; eventually foredunes joined to form a chain. When frequent ferocious ocean gales blew, the sand skipped faster, whipped up the side of a foredune to the very top, then fell precipitously down its back. From there sand traveled inland, in the rhythmic ritual of dune formation. Movement wasn't as constant as in the ocean, but as inexorable. Most geologic formations seem permanent to the human eye, but within the space of a few weeks, sometimes days, wind can change a dune's position. The contour of the dune: transverse, longitudinal or crescent-shaped barchan, may depend on wind currents, as well as native vegetation growing along with them.

To this day the rivers continue to deliver new material; despite modern dams upstream, they still shuttle sand to the sea. Today that section of the Pacific Coast receives a yearly average of only fourteen inches of rainfall, concentrated within a brief stormy season of approximately November through April. In nearby parched hills, native plants adapted for drought conditions do not develop sufficient roots to anchor sediment. Within a short period of time a great deal of sand and soil may still be washed into the bay. The following summer, more sand replenishes the beach.

Along the California coast, earthquakes and the shift of tectonic plates have cast up a steep curtain of bluffs, preventing dune formation. One of the few exceptions, where sand can and does move inland, is the Nipomo area.

Humans came to California, probably from Asia. A thousand years B.C.E. (Before the Common Era), Native Americans known as Chumash swarmed through the dunes, shucking juicy Pismo clams dug from the sand at low tide. Their kitchen middens, piles of white shells, still surface as dunes materialize and disappear. The name Nipomo—almost certainly Chumash—may be derived from their word for village, or perhaps "at the foot of the hill." Although the Chumash were an industrious and inventive people, creating ocean-going plank canoes to trade along the coast, they were hard hit by European diseases and mission culture; by 1850 they were virtually gone.

The first European dune-explorer was the Spaniard Gaspar de Portola in 1769, whose musketeers camped beside a lake they dubbed Oso Flaco (skinny bear). Later, to aid provision-starved missions, they eliminated the local grizzly population.

On September 9, 1850, after Mexico fell to U.S. arms, California became an American state. Rapid economic growth fueled stagecoach routes, steamship service and schemes for real estate bonanzas. The railroad line from San Francisco extended as far south as San Luis Obispo by 1894; four years later Oceano had a handsome dance pavilion and hotel within walking distance of the train station.

For the next sixty years crowds came and went in erratic confusion, lapping up sunshine and band music, then abruptly departing for other shores. Early flurries of wild activity inspired coup-hungry speculators to promote housing subdivisions. But their neat little maps remained maps; dune shifts defied surveying procedures. The most ambitious project was La Grande Beach, between Oceano and Oso Flaco, boasting an ornate Victorian pavilion and a pier to welcome oceangoing steamers. It opened in 1907 and collapsed in a few years for lack of access. By 1915 it was a ghostly shell.

From its abandoned lumber and mortar a hardy breed of scavengers, known as Dunites, built shacks in leafy coves behind the foredunes. Joined by Bohemian idealists under the leadership of Chester Alan Arthur III, the grandson of the twenty-first President, one group launched a humble seaside Utopia. Arthur's adventures, along with those of other colorful characters who lived on the dunes are entertainingly told in Norman Hammond's 1992 book *The Dunites.*

In 1923 the Dunites had unexpected company. Paramount Pictures, filming the silent *Ten Commandments*, chose to cast the dunes as both Egypt and the Sinai Desert. A facade of the temple of King Ramses III was built. Then a causeway was constructed across the Guadalupe section of the dunes so chariot wheels wouldn't sink into the sand as "Egyptian" actors pursued the "Israelites." Garbed in riding breeches, Cecil B. DeMille hoisted his megaphone to command Moses himself to point south toward Point Sal where the mighty Pacific Ocean stood in for the Red Sea. After the shoot, Paramount decided it was cheaper to bury the sets than to haul them back to Los Angeles, creating a windfall for archaeologically-inclined movie buffs who still haunt the area, hoping to discover some discarded trinket touched with star dust.

By the early 1960s the dunes were invaded by a mechanized army of belching two- and four-stroke engines. Dune buggies, mostly home-made contraptions assembled by talented mechanics, foreshadowed the development of commercial All Terrain Vehicles. Their tires shredded the local flora, their drivers frightened campers and fishermen.

As a place to scratch out a living, the dunes had proven at best inconsistent. By the 1960s, at the behest of business and petroleum interests, the whole dune area in San Luis Obispo County was zoned M2, a designation reserved for California's roughest, grubbiest heavy industry.

A BIRTHDAY SURPRISE

"I WANT TO LEAVE EARLY, MOTHER. Just pack a picnic lunch."

Kathy Jackson looked up from her portable green typewriter. "Not too early. Dawn is for roosters, Carol. I'm a night owl—with a stack of letters to write."

"For once, let the Sierra Club stagger along without you. You promised, Mother. For my sixteenth birthday. Anything I wanted to do . . ."

Kathy nodded. "And where do you plan to go?"

Carol put a warning finger to her lips. Blonde with promising contours, she bore no resemblance to the spare, tiny woman with wavy auburn hair hovering over the well-pounded Hermes. There was a good reason for this disparity. All five of the Jackson children were adopted.

Carol grinned. "That," she said, "is a surprise."

"Fair enough." Kathy was open to surprises, having pulled them herself for decades: there was a solo trip through Europe at age eighteen, marriage after a brief engagement to a dashing Persian fighter pilot. She had flown kites from the rooftops of Rangoon, scribbled sketches of peasant life in India, disguised herself in a full muslim burka to travel incognito as a deck passenger, tutored in Teheran. Her Persian marital adventure, often rocky, had long since been discarded, but her emotional volatility had not. She worked her way up from the steno pool into the hurly-burly of the NBC entertainment world of New York and Hollywood. After a series of free-wheeling romances with men of scapegrace charm but dubious social standing, she had startled her friends by tripping to the altar with rich, conservative Duncan Jackson, apparently mesmerized by his mastery of Chopin on the piano.

When Duncan's Santa Barbara family charged him with managing their 13,000 acres of almond trees near Paso Robles, Kathy's ménage, swelled by the quintet of adoptees, moved north. During the marriage she returned to an early love never quite forgotten: nature. Trekking with members of the Sierra Club, mostly in rugged masculine company, she listened with awe as powerful, influential people described their efforts to save wild lands ever more threatened by industry and greed.

Sadly, she discovered after several years of marriage that she and Duncan shared a passion for music and little else. Were it not for their houseful of adopted children—now in their teens—there was little to hold them together. Accordingly she threw her abundant energies into enjoying and protecting the natural environment, an interest since she hiked with her father as a child in the hills above Santa Barbara. Rising rapidly to prominence as an officer and activist in the national Sierra Club, she organized meetings, fired off hundreds of letters, and led strenuous backpack expeditions into wilderness areas of the nearby Los Padres National Forest.

Her full-time hobby had served her well. At 54 Kathy was pink-cheeked and trim, bright of eye and nimble of limb. Despite her five-feet-two height she could keep pace on the trail with anyone. And she was socially flexible, a warm colleague and responsible mother. If her take-charge briskness struck some as disconcerting, it was softened by a transparent honesty; people sometimes disagreed with Kathy, but they were rarely angry at her.

Now Carol promised a surprise. "Okay, birthday girl, up front!" Unlike most families, the Jackson children were all about the same age; but like their peers they were sometimes companionable, often competitive. Kathy blinked into the hot morning sun as she steered her Ford station wagon out of the garage. Morning, as scheduled, had arrived in Paso Robles. Inland thirty-six miles from the coast, the balmy dawn was working toward a scorcher.

Absent, of course, was Duncan. Paunchy, balding, impatient with teen commotion, Duncan preferred the pleasures of the great indoors. Carol was not one of his favorites. He was proud of Kathy's Sierra Club connections but when he accompanied her on one of their trips, he ensconced himself at the nearest luxury hotel while she headed up the trail to sleep under the stars. He preferred to stay home, enjoying the amenities of Janny House, their restored Victorian mansion, a gracious showplace where they entertained people from miles around. From his desk in his high-ceilinged office he could gaze east toward the almond groves, and worry about them. Some trees were dying—victims of a several years' drought.

He thumbed his everpresent stack of three by five "to do" cards—not very thick today. With the house blissfully quiet he would find time to practice on one of his two Steinways, or work on his model train set-up.

Carol ordered Kathy to drive south out of Paso Robles; they headed down old California Highway 101—then a two-lane road—toward the steep Cuesta Grade. Kathy hoped they were headed for someplace cool.

She watched Carol from the corner of her eye. Her daughter's blonde hair, cut to chin length, swirled around her head. Her sweet personality attracted friends. Kathy wondered if her choice of destination had anything to do with showing off her new two-piece bathing suit to her party guests. In the back seats the kids chattered and sang.

Did Carol want to go to the beach? Or maybe inland into the cool stream of Lopez Canyon? She gave no instructions to turn, not even when they passed the San Luis Obispo junction to Morro

Bay Rock—always a favorite with teens. As they neared the town of Pismo Beach, Carol leaned forward. "Turn here, Mother, turn here." So that was it. Carol had planned her party for Pismo Beach, famous for clams. It was probably that *Gidget* movie. All the girls wanted to be Gidget going to the beach.

As the salt air invaded her nostrils Kathy felt a jolt of excitement. She hadn't been to the beach for a long, long time—probably because she had been so concentrated on the Sierras, on the plight of redwoods and the endangered Dinosaur National Monument.

Pismo's morning fog had burned off; the sun was bright so the kids should have a wonderful time. They tumbled out of the car, shouting with glee, running toward the water as they stripped off their shirts and jeans. One of the boys pulled out his enormous, prized "portable" radio from which Elvis Presley blared battle against the roar of the Pacific Ocean. Elvis was losing. She knew at this point the best thing a mother could do for a teenagers' party was to get out of the way.

Kathy, always restless of foot, looked south along the beach. A spot of solitude would be nice. "Don't go in over your knees," she shouted, although she knew that advice would not be heeded, "I'm going to take a little walk down the beach." Carol watched her mother grow smaller as she sauntered into the distance.

As her feet scrunched along in the sand, Kathy suddenly pulled her shirt collar close to her neck She felt uncomfortable, naked. Why? For good reason: she realized she was hiking but she wasn't wearing her Sierra Club "uniform" with its name tag on her hat, flat tin cup at her waist. Most of all she missed her walking stick. Now here was a nice piece of irony! Kathy never felt naked when she *was* naked. On High Sierra trips she thought nothing of stripping to the buff and jumping feet-first into a cold mountain pool, regardless of who was watching. Why did this feel like a Sierra Club outing?

A breeze tickled her ears. The insistent rise and fall of the waves had an orchestral timbre, gentle and remote; not the thunderous roar of Beethoven, but the serenity of maybe Haydn. No. Of Debussy. Definitely Debussy. She wished Duncan would play the French impressionists more often but he had stopped as soon as he found out she liked them.

Beneath her feet a few grains of dry sand whizzed past her ankles, headed inland on the light breeze. In the distance, as if awaiting her arrival, loomed several huge mounds of oddly sculptured sand. Ah yes, the legendary dunes of the central California coast. She had passed them when she drove between Santa Barbara and Paso Robles, but always from an unrewarding angle, with her eye fixed on some other, farther destination . . .

She quickened her stride, made her way around a bend. Now she had the dunes in clear focus. How far they stretched! How they shimmered, danced, sparkled, weaving a carpet of lemony gold along the shore!

And what a benign setting to frame them! In days to come, squiring some influential visitor through the Nipomo Dunes tour, Kathy would pray to be spared the "pouring fog" that often chilled the area. On this August 23 of 1961 she needed no prayer. The dunes shone in full splendor, as if eager to impress their future protector.

Kathy wondered why it had taken a daughter's birthday to bring her back to the beach. Her thoughts turned to another birthday, her own ninth at Carpinteria Beach near Santa Barbara when she had tumbled into a muddy creek to emerge bedraggled, humiliated, an object of noisy derision. It was cruel to laugh at a child on her birthday. She had hated not being taken seriously. She still does.

The farther she walked, the more she was enticed by the soft, rolling mounds of sand that seemed to be mystical extensions of the ocean's waves. She had never seen such a happy ocean/shore connection. A lover of plants, she recognized flowers she had encountered on trips into the Sierras; but these plants seemed smaller, perhaps adapted to the salty coastal environment. What were these beautiful blue ones? Later, she would learn they were named Woolly Blue Stars. Their roots must be helpful in stabilizing the dunes. Kathy smiled; the plants criss-crossed in a pattern, like decorated snoods atop an actress's hairdo. She raised her eyes. The sheer scale of the scene was overwhelming. Empty spaces spread in dizzying array to the horizon, like the virgin expanse of wilderness areas in the High Sierras. Kathy stared. The parallel was obvious. The majestic monuments of sand, whipped by wind and rain into fantastic patterns, were spiritual cousins of the giant sequoias farther north, equally unique, equally irreplaceable. Who but a generous God could fashion such beauty? And who could ask for a nobler mission than to preserve it?

Kathy wanted to cry—her instinctive reaction to any strong emotion—but fought back the impulse. In public appearances on behalf of the Sierra Club she had steeled herself to a rigorous calm, lest she be accused of falling apart "just like a woman." Before an audience she ignored the pounding of her heart, the tears begging for release.

But now they burst from her eyes, coursed down her cheeks, dropped into the sand. And she let them pour. She sobbed, but not in sorrow. What was happening? Why could she weep over the beauty of granular heaps of sand when she hadn't shed a single tear over her vexations with Duncan?

Slowly, she began to recognize the emotion. It was love, and wasn't she something of an expert about that? Hadn't she been there before? Many times. But that was with people, and never as powerful as this.

Calmer now, she found herself breathing, deeper and deeper. Carried away by the clean salt air, the bounding waves, the panoramic dunes, she was almost in a trance when—WHIZZ, a stripped-down VW bug sped past her left ear, nearly knocking her over. Three roistering riders tossed a beer bottle at her feet, bellowed with laughter, and showered sand in her face as they peeled off down the beach.

Kathy stooped to retrieve the bottle. Obviously some people saw the dunes with different eyes. But education could work wonders. She believed that people just needed to be taught what was right.

From that day on she was obsessed.

Carole watched her mother come into focus as she trudged up the beach, "Did you have a nice walk?"

Still misty-eyed, Kathy replied: "Those sand dunes are incredibly beautiful. I think that I must learn a lot more about them. But this is your party."

"That was it, mother. I wanted to surprise you, to show you these dunes. I thought you would love them."

She loved them.

NOT ON MY DUNES

TIRED AFTER RETURNING FROM A DAY on the dunes, Kathy hung up her jacket and dusted off her hat. In the months after Carol's birthday she had enlisted enthusiastic members of her Santa Lucia group of the Santa Barbara chapter of Sierra Club to explore the swoop and sweep of the dunes. On official and unofficial hikes they swarmed like scouting parties of resolute ants, learning dune contours, delighting in the discovery of everything from fields of flowers to cricket tracks. All agreed they should work at turning bureaucratic wheels toward the direction of a scenic area State Park. On January 1, 1962 she led the first Sierra Club New Year's Day trek from Oso Flaco Lake onto the dunes—an event destined to become an annual ritual.

Energized but exhausted, she kept her home front functioning smoothly. Michael, Gay and Carol were preparing dinner—as per her posted instructions. The twins, Larry and Lureen, were off at Judson, an Arizona boarding school—where seventeen-year-old Larry was a safe distance from Duncan's intermittent wrath. She had poured herself a drink, wondering how many Duncan had already consumed. Duncan was riffling through the newspaper, hunting for news of an impending duplicate bridge tournament.

"I need to see if the notice of our hikes got in the paper, Duncan. Hand me the local news."

"You can have the whole paper—when I'm through with it."

"Why don't we get *two* newspapers? Then we won't have to fight over it."

"Can't afford it." He was careful with a dollar, but unpredictable about just where his thrift might surface. He might spend $75 for a locomotive for his model train set-up (which the children were never allowed to touch), but quibble about the price of a candy bar. "Hey, wait a minute! You can forget about your dunes. PG&E just *bought* them. They're going to build an atomic power plant there!"

"What?" She ripped the paper from his hands. With shock she read a very small announcement—the largest power company in the state had bought 1100 acres of land from the Unocal oil company, in the heart of the dunes. She immediately had visions of towering vent stacks, of unsightly transmission lines, of forbidding *No Trespassing* signs.

"No, they can't do that! I won't let them." She read and re-read that three inches of cold, hard type—knowing even as her stomach churned that her entire world had just turned upside down.

"Kathy, it's time you quit playing in that sand pile. You can't take on PG&E. They've got lawyers, engineers, bankers. Besides, I have a hunch the people of San Luis Obispo County will get behind that plant. Think of the taxes they'll get. You can't buck PG&E *and* City Hall."

"No, no, no. Those dunes must be preserved. They are unique, beautiful."

"Kathy, don't you know what people think of you? That you are a little lady in white tennis shoes, tilting at windmills. I won't let you humiliate yourself." Kathy felt her face redden, her stomach tighten, her eyes fill with tears which she quickly willed away.

Dinner was consumed in near silence. Kathy was not accustomed to receiving ultimatums from Duncan. She respected him in some ways—he was a good business man. And she would have to grant that Duncan had put up with quite a lot from her. Generally, he supported her efforts—especially after he met the important people she knew in the Sierra Club, like Bob Cutter from Cutter Laboratories, David Brower, Dr. Tom Jukes. But the club's business took her all over the state, leaving him alone with the kids—only two of whom he liked—and the cleaning woman. A couple of times a year she loaded Santa Lucia officers into his big Cadillac for trips north to meetings in San Francisco.

She accounted herself an adequate wife, only occasionally feeling guilty about her flirtations on the club's High Trips which were sponsored to stimulate and educate the elite of its membership. Duncan was so cold. One Fiesta celebration, always held in August when they lived in Santa Barbara, she had gone to a great deal of trouble to dress herself for a lavish party they were hosting, complete with strolling musicians. When she descended the staircase she expected him to tell her how lovely she looked. When he said nothing, she burst into tears.

"What's the matter now?"

"I worked very hard to please you with my costume."

"You cannot *ask* for my affection," he replied icily. She felt justified in reaching for occasional affection along the trail.

She still thrilled to remember how one favorite companion filled his flat Sierra Club cup from a waterfall, lifted his eyes to hers and said, "I would rather toast you with pure Sierra water than any girl I know with champagne." Yes, she enjoyed her mountain adventures.

Still reeling from the news about PG&E, Kathy resisted the urge to dash for the telephone or typewriter. She needed to think.

When he fell into bed Duncan quickly snored the sleep of a man who drank too much, leaving her to quarrel with her bedcovers while unbidden memories raced through her mind . . .

About her father, William Russell Goddard, whose Yankee accent betrayed his Massachusetts roots. In 1906 he was sent to California by the Young Men's Christian Association to found a new affiliate in a small coastal town called Santa Barbara. Willie's first wife and son had died in childbirth; his surviving daughter

Elizabeth, along with his pregnant second wife, Nellie Sartoris Carr Goddard, moved to Sacramento where Goddard was to be trained in anticipation of his new responsibilities. He quickly became enchanted with California, its scenic vistas, its open possibilities. On July 2, 1907, Nellie gave birth to another daughter who was named Kathleen. Willie was relieved to know that mother and child were doing well, but there was little a father could do now. He had been impatient for the birth because he planned a bicycle trip through Yosemite with some fellows from the Y. Two days after her birth Willie charged the hired nurse to take good care of his girls, then departed to explore the fabled Sierras.

When the time came, the family sailed by coastal steamer to Santa Barbara where Willie Goddard founded the new YMCA in an old adobe house at the intersection of Chapala and Carillo Streets. Soon two more daughters were born.

Father Goddard, a strict Congregationalist, hauled his family to obligatory Sunday services; Kathy fidgeted in her pew, consoled that the afternoon would be better. Most Sundays Nellie threw food into a basket then off they walked to Mission Canyon for a picnic. Kathy's younger sisters, Marguerite and Bernice, preferred to paddle in the creek while their mother read a book—usually one about travel. Besides, her mother was particularly protective of little Marguerite, whose attacks of asthma sometimes caused Kathy to be jealous of the attention her sister received.

But Kathy in her white middy hiked with her father up, up, up above the hills. Always they had to get to the top of something. That was their goal.

She remembered the day some neighbor children were visited by their Aunt Maud from Boston who led the little girls up into the hills. When Kathy gathered wildflowers to present to the stately, dignified old maid she looked at each carefully then identified them by their names, "Why that's Brodiæa." Kathy had called them Blue Dicks. Flowers had beautiful names! She could call each of these wonderful plants by a special name. It was like finding new friends.

Father was rigid. When teenaged Bess ran away from home and, lured by the movie industry, appeared briefly as a child star, Father Willie thundered to his younger daughters, "We will all forget Bess. She has gone to the evil place, Hollywood." When a controversy arose over whether boys should be allowed to use the YMCA pool tables on Sunday, he was adamant. Absolutely not. Despite Nellie's pleas that he should not leave a dependable job, he quit rather than compromise. For a while, Willie Goddard went to State Street every day to hand out religious tracts.

Genteel Nellie was mortified—Nellie, who urged good taste in all things. Nellie, who secretly allowed her daughters to take dancing lessons, "Now your father doesn't approve of dancing. But I believe that Jesus Christ approved of dancing but he would want you to dance in good taste." Kathleen liked to go calling with her mother. She learned to be polite, to sit patiently through boring conversations, swinging her legs, anticipating cookies. Above all, she tried to obey her mother's admonishment: "Don't be saucy."

Forced to realize his evangelism would put no food into little girls' mouths, nor pay the mortgage on the house they built on Prospect Street, Willie went into the laundry business, first at the Potter Hotel until it burned down on April 14, 1921, then with a partner at another location.

The best thing in grade school was Camp Fire Girls. Kathy was to choose for herself an Indian name. She selected *Ulu*, meaning oak in the Chumash language—she loved oak trees. She learned to camp, to cook out-of-doors, to hunt for and identify animals and insects. Kathy began to write little stories; her mother sent them to the Santa Barbara newspaper's children's page called "The Sunny Side Club." Several were published. Although mother was proud she cautioned, "Now you must never become a poet because they don't make a living."

High school was a frustrating time for Kathy. Wiry, active, she was blessed with abundant auburn curls that refused to settle into a flapper bob. The boys noticed, and she noticed them, despite the frowning presence of her father. Ambitious in school, she became the first freshman to win the silver Barry Oratory Cup—talking came easily to her. Although she was elected as an officer in numerous clubs she was jealous of girls she thought were really popular, who got the lead roles in school plays, who were class officers.

At 6:44 on the morning of June 29, 1925, just after she graduated from high school, Kathy was awakened when her bed swayed. The house was filled with the clattering of objects even as her father screamed to get out of the bed and out of the house. A great earthquake had shaken Santa Barbara. Thankfully, the house was not severely damaged—although it slipped down the hill a little. Others weren't as fortunate; thirteen people died. She spent the rest of that summer helping the Santa Barbara City Librarian classify the books snatched from the jumbled library. Many mornings people brought armloads of flowers to the library; she was charged with their arrangement, a duty she came to love.

One day, at her job at the temporary library, an older gentleman asked for Upanishads. Dr. Alexander Irvine was a minister, known to her father and trusted by him; his specialty was comparative religions, a subject which interested Kathleen. His message of tolerance found eager ears. So when the 63-year-old preacher invited Kathleen, then a first year student at Santa Barbara State Teacher's College located in the Riviera area near her home, to accompany him to Europe her parents allowed her to go—assured because two older women from San Francisco were going, too. He hinted broadly that he had connections with a writers' club in London, one where she might be fortunate enough to meet George Bernard Shaw. On the Cunard voyage to England he lured her to his cabin, tried to kiss her and exposed himself. She was disgusted. As soon as they arrived in England she complained about a plantar's wart on her foot that needed medical attention, thus separating herself from the group. Indeed a physician did minor surgery. Then she proceeded to enjoy the English countryside by herself for a couple of weeks, then traveled on to Holland, Germany and Italy with the goal of Florence because she wanted to see the Gilberti doors. Each night, she moved a piece of furniture against her door and put a glass of water atop it—certain that if anybody tried to enter the racket would wake her up. She was perfectly safe.

When she returned to California she enrolled in Mills College, a well-regarded women's school in Oakland. Her assigned room-mate was an intriguing girl named Marzia Nabil-Khan—the dark, slender daughter of a Persian carpet dealer and a proper Bostonian lady. Kathleen was the object of attention from boys from Stanford, of course, but in the roaring twenties girls were beginning to explore new horizons. One way was by looking into the comparative religions expounded by traveling gurus. In those days lecturers from India traveled all over America, describing the plight of their people under the British Raj. Syyud Hosain spoke beautiful English with a golden tongue. Fascinated, the fledgling writer in Kathleen was inspired to write anonymous letters signed "Nadia." One day in the Mills library where she worked she read an Atlantic Monthly article entitled "The Cowardice of Anonymity," whereupon she immediately dropped Hosain a note, revealing her status as a Mills coed. She received a fast telegram in reply, inviting her to dinner. She agreed to meet him; after a few trysts he intro-duced her to the world of sex. More curious than smitten, she rev-eled in the knowledge, "Now I am a woman." She found the expe-rience positive.

A faculty member named Cedric Wright, violinist and photog-rapher, prominent in the still youthful Sierra Club, noticed the girl whose auburn curls always seemed dangerously close to anarchy. Wright's career and personal life were in tatters. Arthritis was forc-ing him to give up his career as a violin teacher at Mills; his wife had left him for another woman. He introduced Kathy to his best friend, the not-yet-famous photographer Ansel Adams, who invit-ed them to a San Francisco loft. One memorable evening Adams played the piano, Wright the violin, Ernst Bacon the cello, Virginia Adams sang. Later one of the men—she was pretty sure it was

Ansel Adams—took off all of his clothes to dance in moonlight pouring through the skylight of the studio while Aaron Copland played the piano. All of this was pretty exciting to a girl going to a proper school like Mills.

To her astonishment, Wright proposed marriage. Flattered—she was barely twenty—she at first accepted. Wright was thirty, Jewish and had a child. He came to visit her family in Santa Barbara during the Christmas holidays. One night they stood bathed in moonlight on a bridge near the Indian Dam in Mission Canyon. As gently as she could she explained why she had changed her mind. "I am a butterfly. I want to see all of the forest. I want to see all of the flowers. I want to know other men. I want to finish college."

Cedric replied, "I have explored the forest. I have found a pool in the center of the forest. I am sitting by the pool and reflecting on the beauties of life. I have explored and I can help you."

"No. I want to go alone."

Her roommate Marzia became her fast friend; through her she first became acquainted with the Bahá'i religion. On a visit to the Nabil-Khan rug store in San Francisco she met an intriguing fellow named Ali Shirazi Parvaz, who asked her out. After that first date, Kathy decided that the dark, mustached Middle Easterner was just a little too slick. Who was he? What kind of family did he come from? So violent was her reaction that she wrote a note to Ali's best friend, detailing why she wanted nothing more to do with the fellow. Unfortunately, Ali found the note and read it. Incensed and insulted, he demanded the opportunity to see her again, to defend himself from her charges. Chagrined, embarrassed, Kathleen agreed to go out with him.

To her surprise, he whisked her off to a San Francisco restaurant every Mills girl dreamed of, Julius' Castle, where she marveled at the panoramic view, was wined, dined and treated to Ali's extraordinary sales technique. First, he recited his family's ancient, honorable lineage, and bragged of his service as a pilot for the British in World War I. Then, in very short order he made her a proposal that was almost businesslike. "I know you, Kathleen Goddard. You want to travel, to meet important people, to have adventure. I can give you all of that. You have great skills with people. In return you will entertain, will create a welcoming atmosphere for the important people I need for contacts in the business world."

Then he dangled the bait. "Tell me, if you could have one wish in the world, one single thing you would want to do, what would that be?"

Surprised, wide-eyed at the door Ali was opening she dreamily replied: "To meet the great poet, Rabindranath Tagore."

Although Ali was only dimly aware of the Nobel-honored writer he replied, "And so you shall."

The opportunity was more than she could resist; just a few weeks later they were married at the home of her mother and father in Santa Barbara.

He did not take long to deliver on his promise of adventure. In 1927 the world was agog over Charles Lindbergh's trans-Atlantic flight. Suddenly everybody wanted to grab headlines with a spectacular flight. Ali's idea was to buy a plane and fly it to Iran, to call it the Persian-American friendship flight. Kathleen, smitten, learned to read charts, to navigate. Ali bought a bi-plane—but on a practice flight near Washington, D.C., he crashed it on the roof of a hangar. Ali emerged unscathed, Kathleen burned her hand on the plane's exhaust pipe, the airplane was a total wreck.

Their finances in ruins, that same autumn she and Ali chose an inexpensive vacation, backpacking through New England. They marveled at little lakes called tarns which were covered with varied golden leaves that looked like coins sparkling in the sunshine. Those days were among her happiest memories of time with Ali.

Ali decided to send Kathleen to meet his mother in Rangoon. Kathy would embark from San Francisco, he would follow a couple of months later as soon as he could wind up his business of selling fire extinguishers in New York City. Her first stop was Hawaii, where she had a few days to explore the tropical paradise around Honolulu. Then it was on to Japan, where she looked up in awe at Mt. Fuji. She stopped at Hong Kong, too. Male passengers on the ship were more than attentive to the pretty little woman traveling alone. Kathy had studied a few Farsi phrases at New York University. But they didn't prepare her for the greeting she would receive from Ali's mother, a silk-swathed woman who sat on an enormous rattan chair, her fingers and arms elaborately decorated with henna. She smoked a huge cigar. She waved off Kathleen's attempt to shake her hand because the American girl was, after all, *pariah*—unclean. Very little progress was made until Ali arrived, whereupon his mother arranged for a Muslim ceremony to cleanse the couple and correct the situation.

Then it was on to India, where Ali planned to conduct business out of Delhi. In the early morning, before the heat oppressed their efforts, the couple went to a riding academy. Ali rode a horse round and round the same course that she preferred to walk. Afternoons found her playing tennis. Usually her friends were the half-British, half-Indian products of the Raj.

Ali delivered on his rash promise. He somehow persuaded Rabindranath Tagore, recipient of a 1913 Nobel Prize for Literature, to grant them an interview. They traveled by train and cart to his estate, Santiniketan in Bengal, where the awe-struck American girl, for once, found herself at a loss for any but the most pre-rehearsed words.

Kathy suspected that Ali was cheating in his dealings, and it was not long before Ali's business practices ran afoul of the British Raj. He was ordered out of India, given a deadline with the threat of jail if he did not comply. The couple soon found themselves in a jam. There were no cabins to be had on the packet headed out of Bombay for Bandar-e Bushehr. European women were not allowed to travel as deck passengers. And yet, Ali might be imprisoned if they stayed. Clever Kathleen devised a plan. She would purchase a

Bourka covering her from head to toe and travel as a deck passenger. The only way she could see out was through a slit for the eyes covered by a golden lattice. She argued that the only really difficult part would be for her to keep her mouth shut. Thus she began an adventure she would later write out in a 600-page manuscript entitled *Passage to Persia or by Golden Lattice and Caravanserai.*

She managed to maintain the ruse until they were safely in Iranian waters in the Arabian Gulf. From the coast they traveled by truck, spending nights in ancient inns called Caravanserai en route, to Shiraz—the namesake home of Ali's family. It was there that she began to suspect that he was not as well regarded as he had advertised back in San Francisco. They were not invited to be houseguests of his uncle, a man who barely deigned to grant them but a brief interview. Kathleen was insulted by their brusque reception; she would never learn what ancient family squabbles or feuds might have led to such treatment.

She recorded one memorable roadside scene. *Once a lone camel lifted his head from feeding knee-deep in green and gazed at us, a crimson poppy dangling from his mouth.*

In those days, travelers simply drove up to Persepolis and climbed around on the ruins:

The stone of the ridge behind Persepolis is a black stuff that looks like deep gray shale, but in reality is very hard. . . . The great blocks whose perfect bonding forms the west porch of the winged bulls from Ninevah are superlative examples. So closely are they fitted that at a little distance the whole appears as one, without a hairline mark divergence between the slabs.

But all archaeologists and travelers who have described Persepolis have left out one of the most beautiful things for me. None of them described the view looking outward away from the ruins toward the distant mountains. . . The clouds were very white. The rain had ceased. . . . Far, far away were the blue mountains, and then mountains that were capped and covered with snow that seemed to melt into the sky where the clouds wound in and out among them like floss along a distaff. The valley in front was a carpet of gold and green.

In Teheran, Ali offered his services to help build a national air force. Rebuffed, he started trading in Palestine, Bahrain and other gulf countries. Kathleen was incensed to learn he often cheated his customers. When she objected he replied: "If people choose to believe me, that is their problem." She could not fathom such an attitude.

While he was off buying goods, she taught English and made friends. One student invited her to spend a summer vacation in the Bakhtiari mountains with the four wives of a local landowner. Although she treasured such experiences, continued friction with Ali dulled her enthusiasm.

When the marriage to Ali limped back into New York in 1931 they separated. Faced with making a living she took a shorthand course, brushed up her typing and got a job in the NBC steno pool. Charged with opening other people's mail she learned a lot about how publicity works: news releases, phone calls, personal visits, follow-up. She advanced to ladies' programming under Margaret Cuthbertson—where she composed news releases for newspapers. It was a fascinating job where she met Edna St. Vincent Millay, Norman Cousins, where she was able to listen to Toscanini conducting the prestigious NBC symphony orchestra. But weekends she found herself hiking with groups sponsored by the New York botanical gardens.

The time had come to separate herself legally from Ali. When she arrived in Reno in 1940 she quickly found a job with an attorney. He chuckled that most of his secretaries lasted only six weeks—the time it took to finalize a Nevada divorce.

When Arch Oboler, one of NBC's stable of star writers, announced his intention to move to Hollywood he insisted that the able, adaptable, cheerful Kathy Shiraz go with him as his right-hand aide. For him and his family she did everything from hiring and firing secretaries, to fending off starlets to killing rattlesnakes who were threatening his baby on the patio. Frank Lloyd Wright was in and out, supervising the house Oboler was building above

Agoura. That was during World War II, when she often had to hitchhike to work or take public transportation.

She was becoming tired of Oboler's frenetic creative impulses. After visiting her parents in Santa Barbara for a weekend, she sat next to a gentleman on the train who introduced himself as Duncan Jackson.

Kathy had a way of encouraging people to open up to her, to reveal their inmost secrets. In rapid order she learned that Duncan was attempting reconciliation with his wealthy parents. Duncan's father, Fred Jackson, had been a successful corporate attorney in Chicago. Fred's mother had worked hard all her life. When she retired to Santa Barbara, her dutiful son soon followed with his wife, son and daughter. The elder Jackson set himself up as an investment banker, bought property atop Mission Ridge, built a showplace home and gardens, which he named El Jardin Encantado—the Enchanted Garden. His landscaping was spectacular; Pearl Chase, the doyenne of Santa Barbara architecture, organized garden tours of his estate. His son Duncan was sent to Stanford where he combined the study of business with his true love, piano. Duncan first married Eleanor, his childhood sweetheart and a fellow pianist, a woman who enjoyed full family approval. Longing for a little spice in his life Duncan joined a theater group in Santa Barbara where he became convinced that by marrying early he had missed the sowing of youthful oats. On a trip to Los Angeles he witnessed a dancer, who removed her clothes to reveal the most beautiful body he had ever seen. He got a divorce, married the exotic Donna, was disowned by his parents, tried—unsuccessfully—to make a living selling Otis elevators, only to return home one day to find Donna in his bed—with someone else.

In Kathy he saw a way to pair up with somebody who was stimulating—yet would bring him back into the good graces, not to mention the money, of his parents. Duncan introduced Kathleen to his family; she was quickly fascinated by Father Jackson's gardens, greenhouses and cultivation of exotic plants. In retrospect she realized that she was more drawn to the father than to the son, but it was Duncan she married at the Jackson's mansion atop Mission Ridge in delphinium season in 1946. The Jacksons' house was filled with the flowers; she even had a hat, dress and shoes dyed to match them.

Kathleen was nearing forty so the couple decided right away to have a family; they submitted to the indignities of what fertility treatments were available in the 1940's. Absent conception, they agreed to adopt an "instant" family. Because they were considered an "older couple" authorities were reluctant to promise babies; agencies urged them to look for slightly older children.

One day father Jackson's real estate agent returned from doing business in the little beach town of Carpinteria. Kathleen would reflect later that the "business" was really terrible. Their company was filling in a saltwater slough, tearing down sand dunes, making land for houses and apartments. But in her pre-Sierra Club days she thought nothing of it.

"That evangelist Aimee Semple McPherson's got a tent down at the beach; there's a whole lot of kids." reported the fellow. "Maybe they've got some extras."

Kathy and Duncan hastened south over Ortega Hill, down Linden Avenue toward the beach. In response to their question, a woman attired in a nurse's uniform said: "That little fellow over there eating oatmeal was given to us by his mother."

His name was Michael. "Oh, if I ever had a child from my own body, I wanted to name him Michael," exclaimed Kathy. They snatched up the very dirty Michael, took him to the best children's store in Santa Barbara, bought everything he needed—from crib to soakers—and loved him deeply.

It was a terrible shock when, after a few months, his mother reclaimed him; her boyfriend had children and she wanted to present herself as a doting mother. But she was unaware that Kathy Jackson would utilize every legal remedy at her disposal until his slatternly mother, who had once more tired of the child, willingly turned him over to the Jacksons, and signed the necessary papers. Gay was an infant whose parents married in haste during World War II then did not want to deal with the consequences of their union. Eighteen-month-old Carol's father had abandoned her mother, who soon died in a motorcycle accident. Saddest was the plight of twins Larry and Lureen who were given away in a bar to a couple who abused them. The half-starved, crying children were rescued by child welfare authorities; the Jacksons agreed to take them in. When alarmed social workers realized the burden of this instant family, they persuaded the Jacksons to give a home to fourteen-year-old Beatrice Altimarino Delgado, whose father had been killed in a mining accident in Mexico and whose mother was confined to a tuberculosis sanitarium. Bea was a great help with the younger children, but Bea's mother could not find it in her heart to give permission for adoption. Kathy responded, "All right, we'll introduce her as our borrowed daughter."

Kathy had plentiful hired help to care for the children; moreover, she was an extraordinarily well organized person. For relief from the constant demands of six children she joined a group of local hikers to climb into the hills above Santa Barbara—the same hills she had so enjoyed with her father.

Through the years she had corresponded occasionally with her erstwhile fiancé, Cedric Wright, who had become a famous nature photographer, now happily married. When she wrote of her enthusiasm for hiking, and about her friends' interest in forming a chapter of the Sierra Club, Wright sponsored her admittance into the organization. He then helped her with the first step, which was to form a separate group, under the auspices of the Los Angeles Chapter. Before long she would become the second chairman of the new Los Padres Chapter. Wright let it be known at the national office in San Francisco that he had a protégée, one with brains, organizational ability, enthusiasm, money, social skills and passion. She was invited to exclusive Sierra High Trips where horses and mules carried gourmet provisions, bedrolls and tents from destination to destination, leaving hikers to stroll at their own rate. Originally conceived as a method of training leadership, attendees were invited on the basis of their prestige, generosity, connections, activism and enthusiasm. Around the campfire individual members spoke of their environmental interests, concerns and intentions. Talented members, like Cedric Wright, entertained with music.

One evening in 1956, after a wilderness trip, then President Ed Wayburn asked to speak with her privately. The tall, slender mountain climber came right to the point:

"Kathleen, the Sierra Club has decided to form a new executive arm, to be called the Council."

"What would it do?"

"It would administer individual chapter concerns—disputes, territorial boundaries. That would free up the board of directors to concentrate on environmental crusades, matters of national policy."

"Why, that's a wonderful idea. How can I help?"

"You will be its first chairman."

"Me?" It was as though a bolt of Sierra lightning had struck Kathy along the trail. "But I don't know how to . . ."

"Don't worry. You will have plenty of help from the national office. We need someone with your skills and interest, someone from outside the San Francisco area."

She felt like Cinderella.

Poor Duncan. He was proud of his wife's role in a prestigious national organization, but resentful of the time and attention she lavished elsewhere. But there wasn't much he could say.

Her first big national environmental effort was the Sierra Club's battle to save Dinosaur National Monument from an impending dam, a fight which stretched from 1951 to 1956. For her part, she sat down and started writing by hand: "I am writing 500 letters and I am asking each one of you to write only five." She supplied the names, addresses and phone numbers of politicians or people who were key decision makers in Washington D.C. Bombarded by thousands of letters coming from people around the country, Washington took notice; eventually the dam was stopped. She felt triumphant.

One of the Jackson financial interests was the huge Jackson-Reinart almond business in Paso Robles where, to escape frost, trees were raised on the tops of hills. The almonds, although very small, were just the right size for Hershey candy bars; the company bought the entire crop every year. A crisis impended when the trusted manager dropped dead in an orchard one day.

Father Jackson delegated his son to run the operation, and hoped he was up to it. The family moved *en masse*, found a neglected old Victorian house in Paso Robles, remodeled it, installed a large swimming pool and settled comfortably into Paso Robles. Kathy soon found fellow hiking companions, most of them in San Luis Obispo thirty miles south, and became a founder of the Santa Lucia group—a subdivision of the Santa Barbara Sierra Club chapter.

But what about this fight for the dunes? Duncan was probably right. The people of San Luis Obispo county would see the power plant as a tax source for local commerce and civic improvement—schools and roads.

They were far from seeing the possibilities of the dunes as a unique jewel. She remembered an occasion during one of her first trips to the dunes when she dropped into an Oceano restaurant for a cup of coffee. The proprietor greeted her across the counter, "Hello, the name's Bill. What can I do for you?" She tried to ignore his brusque manner.

"My, this is so beautiful here. These dunes are magnificent. I've never been here before and I'm so impressed! Don't you think it would be great if the dunes were preserved in a California State Park?"

Bill glared back, "The last thing in the world we want here is for the state to come in and make a park. They'd spoil my business and just take over and manage the whole place. No, we don't want to do anything like that."

She was realistic, and knew the dunes weren't for everyone. Scenic, yes, but they were also demanding. To appreciate them a person needed to get out of the car, trudge through soft sand, crash through thickets of brush, risk encounters with ticks and rattlesnakes, but above all to invest curiosity and energy to reap the rewards of solitude, to enjoy vistas of what she always called: "A white, wind-swept wilderness." They weren't for the casual, for the lazy. You couldn't just drive up to one and say, "Yep, I seen 'em."

Yet she knew in her soul that people who like difficult, even forbidding, scenic treasures deserve to have them preserved.

Well, by gosh they saved Dinosaur National Monument, didn't they? She hardly gave Duncan's caveat a moment's thought as she began to formulate a plan. She already knew the editors of the five nearby newspapers, plus the reporters at the radio stations. She knew her county supervisors, her state representative and senator. She would organize more hikes onto the dunes so people could see their possibilities. She would start another chain of letters of influence. She would learn everything she could about nuclear energy, about PG&E. She . . .

She slid out of the sheets, donned a bathrobe and crept down the stairway. The sound of her little Hermes didn't awaken anybody—they were accustomed to hearing it in the night. She clattered her start to the campaign:

```
Dr. Will Siri
Sierra Club/San Francisco

Dear Will,
    An item in today's newspaper promises
to...
```

3

MARSHALING THE TROOPS

EVERY PERSON IN THE CAR CARAVAN following Kathleen Jackson's station wagon knew something was up. She had sent personal notes to her fellow Sierra Club regulars, even made long-distance phone calls from her home in Paso Robles to urge attendance at a "special hike." While the hikes she led were known for their unusual destinations, this had to be different. Notices posted on bulletin boards at California State Polytechnic College, known locally as Cal Poly, drew a good sprinkling of college professors and students from San Luis Obispo. Some members from the Los Padres chapter had even driven up from Santa Barbara, including Fred Eissler who was on the board of directors of the national Sierra Club. Then there were people who had simply seen a notice in the newspaper, wanted to go hiking and were curious. The advertised destination was Cerra Loma.

From Atascadero, Kathy led the cars up a farm road. As usual, she had scouted the terrain by herself, located a parking area and asked its owner for permission to park cars on his property.

Car doors slammed, people hoisted small day-packs onto their shoulders, greeted each other and prepared to follow Kathy Jackson up the hill. It was easy to tell which were Sierra Club members; they were the ones with flat tin cups attached to their belts. Few had bothered to ask why the out-of-the way Cerra Loma was the destination; on a nice day, nobody cared much.

Kathy was clad in blue jeans, a wide-brimmed hat with a flat crown that fastened under the chin, and heavy hiking boots. She had carefully plotted the route through virgin territory before-hand, even fastened a few strips of rags to branches to assure she wouldn't lose her way. They trudged up the hill like a line of disciplined ants, sometimes beating their way through sage bush and oak groves, other times scrambling along craggy outcroppings. Hikers paused occasionally to catch their collective breath. When they did, Kathy asked Dr. Robert L. Hoover to identify various plants along the way.

After an hour, they came to the top of the ridge where she stopped abruptly, and with a sweep of her hand invited her followers to drink in the sight before them. To her relief, the sun had banished the morning fog. Her choice of a viewpoint was having its intended effect; people were not talking, they were just looking at the magnificent golden dunes trending south along the blue waters of the Pacific.

"Now please, sit down so you can enjoy your lunch. I'd like it if you would stay in a clump because I want to talk to you while you eat." It was traditional at Sierra Club hikes that whoever organized an outing had the privilege of teaching, preaching or inspiring while others ate. The custom served practical purposes. No time was lost while people were chewing; matters of great importance concerning local and national club crusades could be aired. Meetings in dull, sterile rooms could be avoided. Members were generally polite; they realized that if someone went to all the trouble to organize a hike, the least they could do was listen. Being held in a captive audience was little enough price to pay for the free entertainment of a day's outing.

Kathy stood at the edge of a bluff, framing herself dramatically against the pristine view. She pointed, "See, that is the southern edge of San Luis Obispo County. Some of you will remember how impressed we were with the sand dunes, where this group had its first walk on New Year's Day. We dreamed that it would one day be a state park. I have just read in the newspaper how PG&E is buying eleven hundred acres down in the dunes, where they want to build a nuclear power plant. I think they called it an atomic power plant. The sweep of the dunes would be broken by tall stacks, fences and "keep-out" signs.

"At first, I just couldn't believe they could do that. But I went to the courthouse and learned that all the dunes in this county are zoned M2. That is the designation reserved for the heaviest industry: the stinkiest, noisiest, most polluting, dustiest, the most undesirable of dirty work.

"I really don't believe that the people who live here understand what incredible beauty exists in the dunes. As a Sierra Club group, it is incumbent on us to teach people exactly what it is they must protect.

"Our great founder, John Muir, fought the battle to save the wonderful Hetch Hetchy Valley of Yosemite Park from being dammed for San Francisco's water supply. He successfully fought to save it every year for twelve years. He won twelve times. But the thirteenth year, he lost the battle. He only lost it once, but when he did Hetch Hetchy was gone. Once a resource is gone, it is gone forever. We never get it back.

"An atomic power plant would restrict access to the beach, to the digging of clams, to vehicles, to horses, to hikers, to fishermen. There are thousands of miles of seacoast in California, but there are only a tiny few places where sand dunes still build, still move unfettered, still hold their wild enchantment. Now we know that California needs electricity and I don't have any problem with atomic power plants. They may help save our rivers from damming and be better for the air than coal or oil-fired plants. But should we allow PG&E to make electricity on our unique, rare, scenic dunes? As David Brower, Executive Director of the Sierra Club says, 'We are not in blind opposition to progress, but opposed to blind progress.'"

"We must dedicate ourselves to saving these dunes. How, you ask? First, we must get the Sierra Club Board of Directors to agree to help us. I have here copies of their address in San Francisco. I want you to write to the president of the board, Ed Wayburn, and to David Brower, asking them to support our fight to save the dunes."

With a flourish she turned once again to gaze out at the dunes, her stance resolute. For a moment, the hikers were silent, fearful lest she break into the tears she seemed on the brink of, respecting her genuine emotion, absorbing the message. Then they applauded, and congratulated her on a fine speech.

Raptly attentive to her every word was Bill Denneen, a wiry young biology teacher at the high school in Santa Maria. He had recently bought a house in Nipomo, and was looking for a way to fit his ideas about nature into the community. This little woman was right. He must join the Sierra Club and help her.

She did not notice that, off to one side, Lee Wilson's big back was stiffening, his eyes narrowing. He nudged his wife, Lillian, who looked back in alarm, pressing her fingers to her lips in warning. Lee said nothing.

Dressed casually in slacks, a sweater around her shoulders for protection from the morning chill, Kathy sat with Lela Burdett at her spacious kitchen table, surrounded by piles of notes and papers.

In Lela, Kathy had found a welcome compatriot: slim, strong, enthusiastic—with leadership potential. Married to Bernard, a California Division of Highways engineer, she had a young son and daughter at home in San Luis Obispo; she devoted her time to Cub Scouts, PTA and the Methodist Church. Lela leaped at the opportunity to visit Janney House, the Jackson's enormous Victorian home in Paso Robles. She envied Kathy's state-of-the-art kitchen, the intercom system that allowed her to page anywhere in the house, the very large swimming pool with changing rooms and a cabana, even a poolside ping-pong table. A woman came every day to help with laundry and house work. Lela's home was, in comparison, modest. But envy did not blind Lela to the oppressive sense that the Jackson home was not a very happy one.

"I'm leaving now," Duncan stuck his head into the kitchen, greeting Lela with a familiar nod.

"Fine. Don't bother to come home for lunch." Kathy did not even turn to look at him, much less offer any sign of affection as she returned to the question at hand. "We need more members, Lela."

"I thought we were doing pretty well in that department."

"No, we will need a lot more people to help us get the word around. That's always been the way with Sierra Club. Get people to go on outings, then educate them to work for causes."

"Like you recruited Bernard and me. Find people who want to hike and backpack, then get them involved. I'll never forget that first backpack trip when you led us into the mountains at Horse Bridge. Remember, you loaned me a pack but it was so badly balanced it almost killed me! I even broke my bra strap fighting with that thing. If it hadn't been for the rest of the group helping me carry it, I don't think I'd of made it."

"But you liked the experience. . . "

"Yes, but I liked it more after we got our Kelty packs."

"Just right." With their anatomically designed frames, since they became available, Kelty packs probably have done more to enhance the backpacking experience than anything since the introduction of topographic maps.

Lela thought of something she had been wanting to mention; "Kathy, do you think everybody in Santa Lucia group will feel the way you do about trying to get PG&E out of the dunes?"

"Of course. How could they not?"

"Well, you know that Lee Wilson really comes down on the side of business. In his electrical contracting work he does a lot of jobs related to PG&E. He's pretty big with Chamber-of-Commerce types."

"But he's a very good Sierra Club member."

"Yes, but he's much more interested in preserving Lopez Canyon than the dunes."

"What bothers me about Lee is the way he speaks. He has a way of talking softly, so I can't hear him. It's like he's trying to say things I won't know about. But Duncan likes Lee because they work together in the Republican party. He can't get over the fact that Nixon lost. Talks to Duncan about it all the time. Thinks Nixon will run for office again. Imagine that!"

"Do you think we'll get much help from your friends in San Francisco? From David Brower and the Board?"

"I hope so. They were very impressed with the letters from our group. I hope they haven't shelved their interest in sea coast preserves now that Congress has approved the Point Reyes and Padre Island national seashores." To Lela's quizzical expression she clarified, "Padre Island is in Texas. Now they are really pushing for wilderness areas to be established within National Forests. Wouldn't that be fine! Just think, entire areas where grazing, mining, roadbuilding or motorized traffic aren't allowed. Only backpackers, along with a few horses and burros, of course."

Lela nodded, "I'm pretty tired of being almost knocked over by motorcycles in the back country."

"Then there's the constant problem with the Redwoods National Park. I've been talking to Ed Wayburn about the dunes, sending him all the information I could get. Will Siri will be the next president, but he's so busy planning his climb of Mt. Everest that I'll have to wait to approach him when he comes back. So far they haven't committed themselves. I don't know how many letters I've written, but we're sunk unless we get Sierra Club approval."

Lela was impressed with the people Kathy knew in the national office.

"But we need something else, big, something that will really pique the imagination of people who think they MIGHT be interested in joining Sierra Club and saving the dunes. Something different."

The considerable space of silence was broken only by the whine of a vacuum cleaner off in the distance.

"Where have you always wanted to go, Lela?" Kathy rose to pour Lela another cup of coffee.

Lela thought a minute, gazed out of the kitchen window toward the inviting waters of the swimming pool and said, "I've always wanted to walk along the entire coast. Every inch of beach."

Kathy caught her breath, "Lela, that's brilliant!"

Then her mind gathered speed like a train leaving the station. "Let's look at a map. I'll bet that we could walk along the entire coastline of San Luis Obispo County. We could start at the Santa Maria River and do one leg each month. Say one Sunday each month. Lots of people would like to do that. Then they'll want to come back the next month. So we can keep them up to snuff on our progress. They'll bring their friends; we can talk about the dunes, get more people involved. Lela that's brilliant, that's it!"

To Lela's look of bewilderment she said, "Leave the details to me. I'll plan it, walk every inch ahead of time, figure the logistics.

"How about a swim?"

Lela thought she'd never ask.

Reporters and ad salesmen looked up from their desks when a determined woman, expensively dressed down to her gloves and a hat, entered the front office of the cluttered newspaper office. The room was festooned with Christmas decorations.

The receptionist lifted her fingers from her typewriter as she recognized the wife of the county Republican chairman; she rose, indicating Kathy should follow.

In a back office a rumpled, shirt-sleeved man was just hanging up the telephone. When he saw his visitor, he hastily stubbed out a cigarette and stood.

Not waiting for an introduction, Kathy revved up her charm as she flashed an incredible smile, full of sweetness and warmth. "My name is Kathy Jackson. From Paso Robles. You probably know my husband Duncan, the Jackson-Reinert company? Almonds?"

Because the phone numbers for Jackson-Reinert filled one entire page on the yellow section of the Paso Robles phone book, everyone was aware of the size and importance of one of the county's major employers.

"Mrs. Jackson. How nice to meet you. What can I do for you?" His enthusiasm was genuine.

"Usually I mail these announcements to you, but I thought it was time that we got acquainted. I was hoping you might put this news release in your paper." She handed him a professionally prepared sheet, complete from its who, what, where, why and how lead in the first paragraph, doubled-spaced, down to the traditional sign-off-30-at the end. He glanced at its headline; it was the announcement of a series of Sierra Club hikes.

"Of course, Mrs. Jackson. Be glad to. People do love hikes and outings. This sounds like something I'd like to do myself."

"Please do, you would be more than welcome."

He had published several of her releases and was always happy to print any community news he could get his hands on. But it was odd that she should hand-deliver it.

"May I say how much I admire the work you do here on the *Telegram-Tribune*?"

"Thank you, that's very kind. It's hard work. Constant deadlines."

"Oh, I can tell. There's something I'd like to talk to you about," she leaned forward, her smile reframed to reflect serious purpose.

"Certainly, how can I help you?"

"Did you know that the pristine beauty of one of the county's most precious assets is threatened?"

Now he knew what was coming.

"PG&E wants to build an atomic power plant on a place of unique scenic value, the Nipomo Dunes."

He sucked in his breath. "Surely you and your husband don't

oppose that power plant. It will do wonders for San Luis Obispo County. Yours is the only objection I've heard. Everybody else has total enthusiasm for the project."

"Oh yes, we oppose it. It would be a disaster to build there. We intend to keep those dunes safe from development."

"Think of what it will do for our tax base! Why, the supervisors are just drooling in anticipation."

"I'm not asking you to take a position. I'm just here to request that when I send you a news release or a letter to the editor, you consider publishing it."

"But of course, of course."

"And you might check with me? If you need to present an opposing view to PG&E's news releases?"

He sighed. "Certainly, I'd be glad to. We always want to present both sides of any controversy. But you'll certainly be fighting an uphill battle."

"Up-dune battle," she replied. It wasn't much of a joke, but he chuckled in reply, politely.

"We're on record as approving the plant. I'm surprised that Mr. Jackson thinks this way. And I can't think of anything that would alter our opinion here at the *Telegram-Tribune*."

"You will change your mind one day. You are known to be a fair person." She wasn't sure that was true, but it was the kind of thing an editor likes to hear. "Now I know that you have much to do. You are a busy man and I won't take any more of your time. Do you have my phone number?"

She stopped to admire a newspaper award for excellence on his wall, fussed over the picture of his wife and children on his desk, then made eye contact with everyone in the outer office as he accompanied her toward the door.

Before she left she spoke again to the receptionist and in rapid order pried from her that she was an Oceano girl, that her father raised broccoli, that she was going to be married to a young man attending Cal Poly, that she liked roses—and invited her to come hiking.

That day Kathy visited four other newspaper offices, as well as two radio stations. Her message was the same—as was the response.

On the final day of the year, this notice appeared in the *San Luis Obispo Telegram-Tribune*:

Sierra Clubbers plan coast walks

Hikes that will cover the entire 87 miles of San Luis Obispo county's shorelines are planned for the 1964 program of the Santa Lucia and Los Padres chapters of the Sierra Club.

The first hike will be Jan. 4.

Those leading the hikes throughout the year will be Fred Eissler of Santa Barbara, Dr. Howard McCully of San Luis Obispo and Mrs. Kathy Jackson of Paso Robles.

"The series is designed to let residents enjoy, study and evaluate one of the county's prime scenic and recreational resources — the shorelands," McCully said. He is conservation chairman of the Santa Lucia Unit.

Hike No. 1, on Saturday, will begin at 9 a.m. on Highway 1 at the intersection of the road to Oso Flaco Lake — about four miles north of Guadalupe.

A shuttle will be arranged with cars in a caravan to the starting point on the beach at Santa Maria River mouth and the San Luis Obispo County line. From there, four miles of seashore and sand dune hiking to Oso Flaco Lake for lunch is planned.

Those who wish may participate in additional hiking in the afternoon. Hikers should bring lunch, water, a camera and binoculars. The public is welcome, Leader Mrs. Jackson may be contacted at 238-4353, Paso Robles, for specific details.

4

THE RUG DEPARTMENT

KEN DIERCKS KNEW TROUBLE WAS BREWING when he was summoned by Vice President Sherman Sibley to the "Rug Department," as lower echelon employees referred to the luxurious office suites on the thirty-second floor of the PG&E building on Beale Street in San Francisco. These were the only offices in the company with wall-to-wall carpeting. The "Rug Department" administered the 25,000 employees who supplied electricity to forty-eight counties including 360 towns in the northern half of California.

In October of 1963, thirty-nine-year-old Diercks, still as muscled and slim as when he played high school basketball, remained a little in awe of the elegantly groomed receptionists and efficient secretaries to the vice presidents. As an important member of the Governmental and Public Affairs office, he was well aware engineers and lawyers ruled the company. Customarily, executives were promoted from within PG&E, not recruited from other companies.

"Good to see you, Ken. How's the family?" Sibley knew Diercks' wife suffered from a mysterious condition which had finally been diagnosed as multiple sclerosis.

"The girls are growing like weeds."

"And the wife?"

"Better lately. Hasn't had the headaches for awhile."

Sibley was in his 50's, a tall fit man with the sharp eyes and

smooth reflexes of an expert fly-fisherman; a little gray was beginning to show at the temples of his immaculately trimmed hair. He
had risen through the ranks, but Diercks was all too aware that
Sibley graduated with an engineering degree from Berkeley; almost
all top executives held tickets from Cal Berkeley or Stanford.

Diercks was from "south of the slot," meaning his family came
from the wrong side of Market Street. More interested in sports
than education, he even managed to flunk Latin at St. Ignatius so
he could transfer to George Washington, a public school with a
great reputation for basketball. He captained the team, but never
quite got over losing the championship in 1942. When he joined
the Army Air Corps that same year as a mechanic, his
Commanding Officer forgave his ineptitude with equipment when
he discovered Diercks could play ball. The C.O. was loathe to
"trade him" to another base so he was stuck in Sacramento for
most of his military career. At war's end he enrolled at San Jose
State for a quarter semester, didn't like it much, then went to work
at PG&E as a mail boy in the accounting department. Transferred
to the Land Department as a "B" clerk, he almost quit in bewilderment at the vagaries of railroad rights-of-way. His bosses, aware
they had a bright fellow on board, mentored his understanding. He
learned quickly, an apt pupil after all.

It was there that Sherm Sibley noticed his broad Irish face, took
him under his wing and served to mentor him as both men
advanced in the company. In the 1950s California passed the
Collier-Burns Act to facilitate a new freeway system; it was an effective document, but threatened to open a miasma of litigation.
Diercks got acquainted with county supervisors, showed a phenomenal knack for remembering names, details, and legal techni-
calities. He was instrumental in negotiating a Master Agreement
detailing how the State Division of Highways and PG&E should
divide costs of relocating power lines in advance of construction.
His knack for spotting sensible compromises was noticed on the
thirty-second floor. It didn't always make him popular throughout

the company, though, because the term "compromise" meant that individual department heads were forced to reshuffle their budgets.

Sibley studied his protégé. "There's a little problem down at San Luis Obispo."

"The new atomic site?"

Sibley nodded. "Something to do with sand dunes. Gerdes wants you to handle it, before it blows up into another Bodega Bay." Robert Gerdes was a formidable figure, held in awe even by Sherman Sibley. Ten years Sibley's senior, he had left PG&E to establish his own legal practice; when he returned it was as head of the law department and later he was elevated to President and thereafter chairman of the board. Nobody went to Gerdes unprepared. If he thought someone was taking too much of his time he would look at his watch. Everybody knew that meant you had exactly two minutes to complete saying what was on your mind. "Most of all, Gerdes doesn't want any Bodega-style protests."

Diercks winced. He had spent a lot of time and trouble trying to get the proper county permits for the proposed Bodega Head nuclear power plant north of San Francisco. At first the project seemed promising. Few people questioned the wisdom of harnessing the dynamic power of atomic energy for peaceful uses; the future of nuclear power looked unlimited. When a woman named Rose Gaffney, who owned part of the property, began attending Supervisors' hearings the press took notice. Sonoma County was trying to take her property by eminent domain. Here was a local ranch woman, a collector of artifacts, someone with no fear of powerful people. Ken Diercks was the only person from PG&E she would talk to. She was joined by a few clam diggers who objected to transmission lines over a sand spit. The dispute crescendoed into a full-scale uprising spearheaded by an upstart young forestry student named David Pesonen; he organized local citizens and Sierra Club members in the Bay Area to write letters to fight the plant.

Forced to reassess their plans, PG&E geologists came to the dismaying conclusion the ground upon which the Bodega plant was to be built sat almost directly on top the San Andreas Fault. Even the gung-ho bureaucats in Washington, eager to develop nuclear power, had to withdraw the blessings of the Atomic Energy Commission from a project so glaringly fault-ridden. So when Robert Gerdes became chairman of the board, his first job was to get PG&E out of upstate Sonoma County as gracefully as possible, then to find places to put more power plants.

Sibley continued, "You know we put millions into Bodega in roads and improvements—money that went straight down the drain. Gerdes doesn't want that to happen again."

Diercks nodded, "I've lost two in a row now. I don't like to lose. Sonoma County hasn't been very good to us. Before that we lost the rights-of-way for transmission lines. Used to be people didn't care where we put the lines, as long as the county got its tax dollars."

"Now they care, Ken. And I can't say I blame them. Hell, I don't like to get up in the morning and see a big blanket of Los Angeles-style smog moving in to smother my family. Clean air is the name of the game, Ken. We're running out of rivers for hydroelectric power. But we've still got the ocean - and the atom. Gerdes wants to kick off the Super Site program with the Dunes at Nipomo."

"What's the 'little problem' you referred to, Sherm?"

"So far, just a solo lady crusader. But she's tight with Sierra Club—which means political muscle. Who do you know, Ken?"

Diercks' mind began to roll through his contacts. At PG&E-sponsored hospitality rooms for convention delegates to the County Supervisors Associations, gatherings of District Attorneys, meetings of the League of California Cities and similar functions, Diercks had become acquainted with a lot of people, especially in the Democratic Party. Occasionally Diercks celebrated with delegates and at times had difficulty finding his way back to his room. In a company full of slide-rule-bound technocrats, Diercks had gained the grudging reputation of being a "political engineer", able to draw upon first-name familiarity with local officials in every one of the forty-eight counties served by PG&E.

He ticked off a few names, "Lyle Carpenter, for one. He's a supervisor. Likewise Fred Kimball. Vern Sturgeon is their state senator. There's a businessman, Mike Hermrick. They should all be friendly to the idea—if only because their economy could sure use it. Who's the female fly in the ointment?"

"One Kathleen Jackson. She's raising hell about those sand dunes. Says there's nothing like them anywhere on earth, etcetera. I understand her husband's big in the almond business in Paso Robles. She's probably one of those rich busybodies trying to make a splash. She's held some office with the Sierra Club, though. Could mean trouble."

"What does Gerdes want?"

"Whatever he can get without another bloodletting. And for this one you'll be on your own, Ken. No need to report back for instructions. Gerdes is giving you full authority to speak for PG&E."

Ken Diercks' back stiffened. Speak for PG&E, a company where "check with the boss" was as automatic as arriving for work on time? A guy from South of the Slot?

"You'll probably straighten it out in two or three weeks."

"Two or three years is more like it, Sherm."

"Think your wife can handle your being away if it takes longer?"

"I hope so, Sherm. I hope so."

"You've got a reputation for straight shooting."

"Without it I couldn't get a dog out of the pound."

"Hang onto it, Ken."

5

THE LUNCHEON MEETING

"AND THIS IS MRS. DUNCAN JACKSON from Paso Robles."
A round of tepid applause followed, as the nearly all-male audience
craned their necks for a look at the fashionable woman beneath a
fetching blue hat, seated at the speakers' table. At public gatherings,
Kathleen was careful to dress, and behave, as the socially
respectable matron she was. She would never dream of wearing her
Sierra Club garb to a social occasion or a government function.

She was not at all sure why she had been invited to the Golden
Tee restaurant in Morro Bay by a group calling themselves Friends
of the Central Coast. Perhaps it was because the guest speaker was
a man from the California State Parks Department. She had a good
chat with him while she picked slowly at her chicken pot pie.

After dessert, Marlboros, Kools, Chesterfields and Pall Malls
were pulled from pockets as the room filled with smoke as thick
as fog rolling in from the Pacific. Kathleen wrinkled her nose;
few of her environmentalist friends smoked, except for the occasional pipe.

The speaker extolled the beauty of California's shorelines, the
necessity to preserve beaches. By then Kathleen had noticed that
many in the audience were realtors; at first they feigned interest,
even though she knew that what they liked to see on scenic coast-
lines was subdivisions. Too much strawberry shortcake was taking
its toll; many a bald head threatened to loll forward into slumber.
She wished she were home at the typewriter, banging out urgent

correspondence. Or better yet off on the dunes, tramping toward some undiscovered delight, such as an unfamiliar wildflower. But nobody would have guessed from her facial expression that she was far afield. Her eyes were focused sideways on the speaker, in apparent rapt attention.

No, she must think of this as an opportunity; she could put more faces to names, perhaps ferret out a sympathetic supporter or two. It was always a happy surprise when an occasional stranger sauntered up, and bent to her ear almost conspiratorily, "Mrs. Jackson, I love to wander on the dunes. I am so happy you are doing something."

As the meeting was adjourned she stood up and pulled on her white gloves in anticipation of greeting a couple of acquaintances as she made her way to the door.

Suddenly her way was blocked by several men, tall fellows she had noticed seated at a table directly in front of the speaker. Something about the superior cut of their suits, the fashionable narrowness of their neckties, had signaled the quartet were from out of town. Apparently they were important; during lunch she had noticed that many local businessmen made their way to the table to shake hands and fawn.

"Are you Mrs. Jackson of Paso Robles?" asked one man, clearly their leader.

"Why yes, I am," she replied with her habitual cheer.

"You're the one who has been putting some items in newspapers about that unpopulated area down at the south end of the county, the sand dunes?"

"Yes, and who are you?"

He looked around at his companions and said, "We are PG&E."

Kathleen's eyes opened very wide as she took their measure. For a moment she seemed to stare, but she quickly recovered her natural poise. "Great. Let's get acquainted. You are . . ."

"Ken Diercks. I'm in PG&E's Department of Governmental Affairs." He extended a hand; Kathleen noted he knew just the right amount of pressure to exert for the occasion. "We would like to come to your home and talk over some things."

"I'd like to talk with you but not at my home and not by myself." She took a deep breath, thinking fast. "I would suggest that you come to a meeting of the executive committee of the Santa Lucia group of the Los Padres Chapter of the Sierra Club. You see we are not yet a full-fledged chapter."

Diercks hesitated, but only for a second. "I don't think that would work out, that might involve too many people."

"Then how about coming to a meeting of our conservation committee, because our concern is a conservation one. These are not only scenic dunes, they're scientifically valuable."

"Well, there again it involves a committee."

She stopped. In turn she looked each man in the eye, smiled sweetly, then said to Diercks. "You are a group."

He had to hand her that one, "OK, just two of us could come."

"Then we would include the conservation chairman, somebody from the committee and myself."

"I don't know," he thought, stroking his chin, and as he did so Kathleen took another measure of the man from San Francisco. Nice looking, fit, obviously informed, quick rather than slick.

Then it struck her. These men had come from the Bay Area with the specific intent of meeting her. For just a moment she felt flattered, then her eyes narrowed slightly, "Have you ever been down to your land on the dunes?"

A bit shamefacedly, Diercks contemplated his well-shined shoes and replied, "I haven't."

She turned to each man in turn and they all shook their heads; they hadn't been there, either.

"It seems to me you really should know what you've got down there; it's just remarkable. I'm going to suggest that the conservation chairman of our chapter and I invite you on a trip down into *your* land."

"Well, we'll have to think about that."

"Yes, let's do it!" Already she was mentally mapping out a route through the choicest area of the dunes.

"We'll go back to San Francisco, and be in touch with you within ten days."

Not ten days, Kathleen thought to herself. I will call and they will come sooner.

6

THIS LAND IS YOUR LAND

"ARE YOU SURE YOU WANT TO GO THAT EARLY?" Kathy was on the phone, arranging to meet Ken Diercks at PG&E's office in San Luis Obispo. "Very well, I'll be there. Oh, and you'd better dress very casually. You'll need good walking shoes on the dunes." She didn't like to get up early; moreover, she was fearful lest the usual morning fog would leave the impression that the dunes were just piles of sand surrounded by bad weather. Because this might be a make-or-break day, she hoped the dunes would show themselves to be so glorious the mighty company men would just slink off and leave them alone. She was going into battle, however muted, and the responsibility unnerved her.

Promptly at nine she presented herself. Although she had arranged for the Santa Lucia group conservation chairman to accompany them, he had begged off at the last moment. Maybe he wasn't up to the task. She would be flying solo. Kathy hoped her hand wouldn't betray her by shaking as she extended it. She was dressed in her full Sierra Club outfit: wide-brimmed hat, flat tin cup fastened to her belt and daypack. Diercks stood tall as he introduced his companion, "Good morning, this is Dick Alvis from our land department."

"Happy to meet you," she said to the slim young land specialist whose return smile was perfunctory. She suppressed a grin when she saw that they sported brand new khaki pants, flannel shirts, and pristine white sneakers; here and there an errant price tag still attached. Their attire reflected a hasty foray through the local J.C. Penney store.

"When we went to breakfast this morning, somebody asked us if we were going on one of President Kennedy's 50-mile hikes!" said Diercks, referring to a fitness craze emanating from the White House; in 1963 everybody was talking about it and quite a few people gave it a try.

He indicated that Kathy should take the seat beside him in his Oldsmobile, Alvis in the back as they headed south out of San Luis Obispo.

"Is Diercks a German name?" she probed.

"Yes, I'm German on my father's side, Irish on my mother's." So that accounted for his broad, freckled face and reddish hair. She always thought of Irish people as having a gift of gab; Germans she thought of as stubborn.

"Mr. Diercks. Do you enjoy the out-of-doors? You look fit."

"Call me Ken. I used to play basketball."

"Tell me about what you do at PG&E?"

"I'm not sure it's very interesting."

"I assure you that I am *most* interested."

She needed all the information she could get. Diercks obliged by telling her about his contacts with government at all California levels: the legislature, county supervisors, planning commissions. It was half an hour's drive to their departure point. Kathy pressed on, "Have you been active in PG&E's proposed atomic power plant at Bodega Bay?"

"Yes, I've been going to hearings before the supervisors in Sonoma County."

"And do you think the plant will be built?"

"It's not in the coffin yet; but we're looking elsewhere."

Diercks was pleasant, chatted amiably but revealed little. Obviously he played his cards pretty close to his chest.

"And what about Mr. Jackson?" he asked, "Is he active in the Sierra Club?"

"No. If he accompanies me to outings, he stays behind in a hotel. But he is proud of my conservation work."

"I understand he is active in the Republican party." She glanced at him, realizing Diercks too was probing for clues.

"Yes, we frequently entertain at our home in Paso Robles. Is there a Mrs. Diercks?"

"Yes. But my wife isn't well." His tone changed; Kathy could see he didn't want to talk about it.

As they neared the farming village of Guadalupe they saw Mexican workers cutting broccoli, cabbage and cauliflower from fields, lifting crates onto the backs of trucks. The smell was pungent, loamy.

They turned down a muddy road in the direction of the ocean; the fog thickened to the point where Diercks had to flick the windshield wiper occasionally to clear it. "Almost like it's raining," he noted. The road was muddy, rutted.

Alvis spoke up for the first time, "Are we on PG&E's land yet?"

Kathy twisted her neck so she could see into the back seat: "No, this is agricultural land. PG&E's is off to the right; there's no road across it. It stretches all the way from Highway 1, across the Southern Pacific tracks, to the ocean. This agricultural road is the only access." They parked, got out, she pulled on a daypack and they tightened shoelaces. An onshore breeze made the fog seem chillier than it was.

When everyone seemed ready, Kathy took a deep breath and smiled as she stuck her hands in her pockets so they wouldn't shake. So much was at stake. "We are a few yards from Oso Flaco Lake, one of at least ten freshwater lakes on the dunes. Believe me there *is* a lake over my shoulder, but you can't see it because it is surrounded by willows. These lakes are fed by Oso Flaco Creek and underground water. This is a natural wetland supporting its own biotic system where each thing is dependent on the next. We have special little creatures wriggling in the water, snakes—" she saw Alvis blanch so she quickly added, "although there are no poisonous ones right here—doves and many other species of birds, squirrels, bobcats, raccoons and of course, fish."

Noting that they weren't hanging on her every word, she turned and marched off crisply down a straight dirt road. Diercks strode purposefully at her side, his eyes taking in everything. Kathy figured he was about twenty years her junior, but wondered if she should slow down.

"This road to Oso Flaco Lake was used by the dune buggy people." Noting a flicker of interest from Alvis, she elaborated. "They build dune buggies by stripping most of the body parts off of Volkswagen beetles, then souping them up. They remove the mufflers so they make an awful lot of noise."

At the end of the causeway she hurried them past makeshift camp sites set up by the buggy people. Their canvas and plastic tents were surrounded by litter, abandoned furniture, beer bottles and cola cans. She frowned but said nothing, turning up a sandy road. On a weekday there were very few campers; however, two or three noisy little machines could be heard in the distance.

"How do you feel about the dune buggies?" asked Diercks.

"Some of them do a great deal of damage. However, their leadership agrees with us that the entire stretch of dunes should be a California State Park."

She thought she heard Alvis say to Diercks, "I thought this land was supposed to be pristine."

As quickly as possible, she turned away from the road, striking up the side of a dune. When they began walking on sand, Diercks and Alvis opted for a macho display by attempting to sprint up the side of their first dune. It seemed that for every step forward, the sand pulled their feet back about six inches. Alvis stumbled to his knee, cursing beneath his breath as his shoe filled with sand.

Kathy turned to him helpfully, "Never hurry up a dune. Take your time, going faster won't help."

Alvis barely concealed his sarcasm, "Never hurry up a dune. I'll remember that." He was already out of breath; Diercks wasn't finding his footing, either. She gave them more tips on dune climbing, recommending they might consider a walking stick in the future.

After a few minutes Kathy paused and pointed down the hill where, between willows, they finally could see Oso Flaco Lake. "That's a pretty big lake!" said Diercks. "It must cover twenty acres." She pointed out ducks, cormorants and terns that dove into the water in search of fish, or chased each other in some kind of mating ritual.

"Would you call it an oasis?"

"Yes, it is actually a riparian area. Those birds in the cattails are house finches somebody let loose. They flourish here."

"What does Oso Flaco mean?" asked Alvis.

"It is Spanish for 'skinny bear.'"

Kathy stooped to snap off a stem topped by a purple flower and indulged in the impulse to teach. "What do you think this is?" Diercks appeared to be a little put out. Was it because she had put him on the spot like a schoolboy? "Well, smell it," she suggested.

Following her example, he crushed a little in his hand. "Maybe like a spice or something."

"Excellent. You would make a good botanist. This is the Dune Mint, *Monardella crispa*. This species grows here, and nowhere else but we see fewer every year. The dune buggies are tearing them up."

On they trudged, each step seemed to require at least twice the normal effort. "I'd rather be on water skis," said Diercks. "Easier on the calves."

She wanted to explain more about the abundant plant life, but resisted the urge to extol the Silver Dune Lupine.

"Are we on our land yet?" asked Alvis. It seemed to be the only thing that interested him.

"No, we are now on Union Oil land."

Although the atmosphere of the dunes was calming her nerves, she couldn't detect that it was having the same effect on the PG&E men. The fog certainly wasn't helping. She wished it would lift, brighten up. Trying to put a good face on the weather she pointed upward, "See the fog rolling in? It reminds me of smoke following a speeding locomotive. We're getting closer to the ocean. You can hear it a long time before you see it."

After another five minutes the little party topped a dune to gaze down at gigantic ocean rollers parading toward the beach in orderly, energetic succession. "Fishermen love this stretch of the beach. They flock here for surf casting." As they approached the water Diercks glanced into a pail where several small live fish swam. "Surf Perch. Delicious, very delicious," said the Filipino angler, proud of his catch.

Kathy stopped to talk with him. She learned the man was from Santa Maria, had six children, worked for the city, came here to fish about twice a month. "I work with the Sierra Club. Would you like to see this area become a state park? So you can always fish here?" She said nothing about an atomic power plant as an option. The fisherman nodded.

Turning to Diercks she predicted, "Some day, recreation will be more important than atomic power."

They turned north. "We are still on Union Oil land, but in a few minutes we will be on yours. Oh look, I believe I begin to see my shadow." Gradually the sun emerged, glorious and intense, intimidating the fog into submission. Dick Alvis shaded his eyes with his hand. "I forgot to tell you to bring hats. Sorry."

Along the beach they strolled. The hard, wet sand left by the retreating tide was easier to walk on. From time to time a dune buggy or a Jeep whizzed by. Dick Alvis' look showed he would like to hop onto one and be whisked away.

She glanced to her right, heading away from the water. They slogged behind her on the looser sand. She stopped abruptly before a concentrated scattering of white shells. First she stood in silence, then dropped reverently to one knee, covering her eyes with one hand. Diercks and Alvis glanced furtively at each other, a little embarrassed. She stood again and blew her nose on a bandanna. "This is an Indian kitchen midden. This is all that is left of the

Chumash Indians' culture, people who once came to the dunes to gather food. They couldn't handle the white man's diseases so most of them died. This is a sacred place. They came before us and they are gone. They should be here still. Can't you just see the women opening clams, spreading them to dry, gossiping and calling out to their little children? It just gives me shivers to think of it." As she found herself on the verge of losing her composure and bursting into tears she squared her shoulders. "It would be a shame if the only evidence of these people were buried forever. Beneath an atomic power plant." Quickly, she turned to start walking again.

Alvis was looking out to sea, studiously avoiding eye contact. Diercks picked up the conversation. "I can tell you like people. Some conservationists seem to be more concerned with trees and animals."

"Maybe some do. But there is no reason to preserve special places except for people—especially those who are not even born yet. We should care more for the people who come after us than we do for ourselves. If we do not accept the responsibility to be stewards of great natural beauty, who will do it?"

"Have you been a Sierra Club member for long?"

"Since 1952. I helped found the Santa Barbara Chapter, then the Santa Lucia group. One day we will be a chapter."

"Do you know people in the national office?"

"Oh yes, I know most of them. I was the first chairman of the Sierra Club Council, set up to deal with internal chapter matters and their territorial disputes. Boundaries and such. So the board of directors can address themselves to matters of national importance, such as the dam at Dinosaur National Monument. The man who is president now, Ed Wayburn, personally asked me to take the job."

"And David Brower?"

"I don't know him well, but of course I know him. He is very inspirational." She began dropping names: Dick Leonard, Will Siri, Peggy Wayburn, Robert Cutter.

"If you would like to talk with any of them, I would be happy to arrange it. It is the most wonderful organization in the world. You should join."

"I'm not much of a hiker."

"Oh, but you don't have to be. All you have to do is care for the earth."

"Evidently all your members don't feel the same way. I met a man named Lee Wilson. He said he would like to see an atomic power plant on the dunes."

Kathy frowned. "We work together in the Santa Lucia group. He hasn't been to the dunes very often. I'm sure he will come to understand their importance." She changed the subject, "Fred Eissler, a member of the Los Padres chapter in Santa Barbara is on the national board of directors. He has been a very great help to me. He is a teacher and feels it would be a great mistake to build an atomic power plant on the dunes."

After a few minutes Kathy stopped, squinted east to spot a familiar landmark, then literally drew a line in the sand with the point of her walking stick. "This is where your land begins."

Slowly, they worked to climb the slip face of a dune. At one point the slope was so steep they dropped to their hands and knees and crawled. Disturbed granules of sand streamed down on either side of their hands; their peripheral vision provided a dizzying optical illusion, like film being run too fast through a projector. It seemed the dune defied their efforts to climb it. Breathless, they finally stood up at the top, gazing back down at the ocean. "Are you trying to make us think this land is too tough to build on?" asked Alvis.

She invited them to sit. She took chocolate bars from her pack, unwrapped them, broke them and passed out small pieces. "Look. You can see south clear to Mussel Rock, where the dunes end."

"The dunes are so vast. Don't you think there's enough of them for your conservation cause *and* PG&E, too?" asked Diercks.

"No. If you build a plant right here, you will split the area clean in two. This is nearly equidistant between Pismo and Point Sal. It would divide the territory physically, and in people's minds. They belong together, as an entity."

"What is the Sierra Club's attitude toward this site?"

"I cannot speak for the Club, but I believe at present their thinking is that if PG&E should decide to use this site, the plant should be placed inland, at least 4,000 feet from the beach."

Diercks reacted sharply. "Why, that's almost a mile. The expense of laying pipes for cooling the reactor would be astronomical. And look, this high dune is in the way. The company thinks 500 feet from the mean high tide line would be plenty. That would put it back far enough to reduce the visibility factor, OK?"

"Not OK," she responded. "But if the plant were 4,000 feet from the ocean, that would put it close to the railroad tracks. Wouldn't that be a convenience, for construction and accessibility?"

"Not necessarily. You know, PG&E has been up and down the coast looking for suitable places to put power plants. They can't be located on top of crumbling bluffs."

Alvis added, "We've been doing preliminary surveys of this site. So far, the engineers say thumbs up."

Diercks continued, "The Sierra Club has made it clear they are against more hydro plants. We think we have a solution to that— atomic power. It doesn't damage the rivers or the air, OK? But there are very few places where there aren't too many people around."

"You should see this beach on a weekend when we have a minus tide. Tens of thousands on the beach, digging for clams. People run into each other in beach buggies. They even have heart attacks!"

"Are you aware of how much pressure we are under to provide more electricity? California's population might even double!"

"But those people will need places to go, to escape from the pressures and smog in the cities."

"Maybe. But when they can't fire up their toasters, we'll be blamed."

She sensed her argument should cease, at least for the moment. She fell silent, hoping the warmth of the sun, the lulling sound of the surf, the buzz of a bumble bee, would create their magic. Her words didn't seem to be helping.

She took out a canteen, poured water into the flat cup at her belt and drank it. The men looked greedily at the water, which she did not offer to share. She seemed oblivious to their thirst. Diercks smoked a cigarette while they swatted an occasional fly.

Dick Alvis was suffering from a blister on his heel where his new shoes had eaten clear through his socks. "No use in emptying out the sand, they'll just fill up again," he complained.

As they looped back toward Oso Flaco Lake, Kathy could see that Diercks' freckles were blotching at an alarming rate. He was in for a terrible sunburn. And the slouch in the men's shoulders indicated they were tiring. She wondered, briefly, if she had taken them too far. From time to time Alvis would ask her to point out exactly where the borders to their land were.

A breeze had sprung up, whipping their jackets full of air, ballooning like spinnaker sails; blowing sand past their ankles, sandblasting them lightly. Now windburn layered pinkness atop their sunburn. "It's pretty windy out here," said Diercks.

"Well, that's what sand dunes are all about," she responded. "You are privileged to see just how a dune is built. Every day is different. If you were to build a power plant, I couldn't guarantee that the sand wouldn't build itself up into a dune and claim it."

Diercks and Alvis were heartily happy when they could see the car. "How far have we walked?" asked Alvis.

"About seven miles," she responded.

"It seemed like more. Like about fifty." He glanced at his watch, and said, "It's past two."

"Now I think that we should go to the Far Western Steak House in Guadalupe and have some soup," said Kathy.

"Wonderful, we would love to take you to lunch."

"No, I will pay for *my* lunch and you may pay for *your* lunch."

"But we insist."

"No, never let it be said that you took me on a trip down to *your* land and then *you* bought lunch, because anything either of us would say later could cause confusion."

Kathy led two very red gentlemen into the high-ceilinged dining room of the Far Western Steak House. The two-story brick building is a Guadalupe institution where the curtains are made from cowhide and the wall decor consists of mounted heads: cattle, elk and deer. Local growers and ranchers gather to discuss the price of broccoli while they wolf down huge slabs of beef. She greeted the waitresses by name. Their expansive shapes and attitudes perfectly matched the portions that would shortly be served. Kathy ordered her own favorite, a bowl of the cook's homemade cabbage soup.

A couple of businessmen, recognizing Diercks, approached their table. He greeted them by name.

They replied, "Glad to see you. We sure are interested in that PG&E power plant. Would you come talk to our Lion's Club?"

Diercks pulled a notebook out of his pocket. "I'll be down next week to talk to the supervisors. Could you work me in then?"

"I'm sure we can. I'll get ahold of the program chairman right away. Why, Mrs. Jackson, what are you up to?"

"I took Mr. Diercks and Mr. Alvis to see *their* land." She smiled; the men had been guests at her home in Paso Robles.

As he sat back, rubbing his stomach and sipping his coffee, Diercks wanted to light a cigarette, but noted that Kathy had not yet finished her soup. "Aren't you hungry?"

"Oh yes, very hungry. But I like to eat slowly and to savor every single bite." Since childhood it had been her custom to eat slowly, a habit some people found exasperating.

Taking advantage of her silence, Diercks said, "You know, don't you, that you may be the only person in San Luis Obispo County who really doesn't want PG&E to build our generation plant here."

"So people keep telling me."

But lulled by the morning's exertion and a hamburger the size of a manhole cover, Diercks once again found himself the subject of interrogation. He did his best to field Kathy's questions, her comments, her suggestions that PG&E should just forget the whole project and go away.

"Isn't there some other place you can build?" she asked.

"We've certainly been looking. There may be no more than ten places such a plant could be feasible on the entire California coast. Nipomo is one of them. And one of the best. Of course there may be other places, but maybe not in this county. How do you think the people of San Luis Obispo County would feel if we put the plant in Santa Barbara County?"

"They wouldn't like it at first. But eventually I would hope that they would understand that the dunes are a great recreational resource, and that will bring people to stay in motels, to eat and to buy things in the gift shops."

Dick Alvis squirmed. Over the course of the day Kathy had figured that he didn't like controversy, was more interested in property lines and geological formations than arguments.

Diercks shook his head, "I suggest you think that over. People are counting on PG&E tax dollars to help pay for schools. You wouldn't be very popular if they lose the power plant. And you might lose the dunes anyhow. With their M2 zoning almost anything could be put there."

The very brief twitch in her chin showed she received his message.

"Now I would like to go back to your office and look at your maps," she said after separate checks had been settled.

Diercks nodded his agreement, Alvis groaned beneath a burp.

At the local office she pored over maps. "Where did you get these?"

"Our land department made them."

"I can see they must have been doing a *lot* of surveying. They are very good maps. Very interesting. Now where does PG&E want to put their plant?"

Alvis pointed out a couple of possibilities. She countered. "But that is a very special willow grove. Red-tailed hawks breed there."

"I'm sure they can find another place," said Diercks.

"Do you know how deep the ocean is, how far your intake pipes would need to be laid? I believe it is very shallow for quite a distance."

"Our people are undoubtedly looking into that." assured Diercks.

"Do you think atomic energy is safe? Fred Eissler doesn't. He thinks it is very dangerous."

"Most studies suggest it can be made perfectly safe."

"I don't know enough about that, but I'm going to find out," Kathy promised.

She took copious notes, wrote down names he mentioned; not until nearly six o'clock did she offer to leave. By that time Alvis wasn't even trying to suppress his yawns; yet Kathy seemed to gain energy as she went along. For Dick Alvis, the day was a unique experience; shortly thereafter Alvis returned to his position in San Francisco and never returned to the dunes.

It was nearly dark when Kathy crawled into her station wagon and pointed it toward home in Paso Robles. From the maps she had just seen, she knew that PG&E had done far more than just talk about building a power plant on the dunes. These surveys were by no means preliminary.

It did seem that she was all alone in her fight against the mighty utility. They could swallow her as eagerly as a lizard grabs a fly. It was up to her to stay one step ahead of the lizard's tongue.

7

BACK AT THE RUG DEPARTMENT

"HEARD YOU HAD A BIG HIKE," Sherm Sibley couldn't suppress a joke at Diercks' expense. "The guys in the land department said you peeled more off your nose than Carol Doda on a Saturday night," referring to a popular Tenderloin stripper.

Diercks smiled. Joking was part of his job, so he could take it as well as give it.

"So, how are things in San Luis Obispo County? I had lunch with a honcho from Union Oil. He doesn't think we'll even need to go through the permitting process. Says everything is zoned and ready to go."

"Not so fast. We've got a problem."

"What do you mean, the Jackson woman?"

"She's another Rose Gaffney. Tough, smart—she evidently learned a lot from Dave Pesonen."

"Is she working with Pesonen on this thing?"

"No. I understand he's in law school. Out of action for now."

"So, what's the problem? I thought you told me the county supervisors were on board. What are their names again?"

"Lyle Carpenter and Fred Kimball are the leaders. They're for it, along with their State Senator, Vern Sturgeon."

"Who else have you talked to?"

"The usual: Rotary, Kiwanis, Lion's Club, Realtors, Chamber of Commerce and oh, yea, the abalone divers. They meet at a bar in Morro Bay. In fact they meet almost every night."

Sibley looked sharply at Diercks. "You're not drinking too much, are you?"

Diercks shrugged.

"And what's the reaction down there?"

"Just about universally, everyone's in favor. Think it's a great idea. Want us to pay their taxes. Build their schools."

"So, what can she do? One woman—"

"After Bodega, I think we've got to pay attention to conservationists. She's really in with the Sierra Club brass and she's tough as nails. Smart, writes well, knows how to work the P.R. game. She may not gather a *lot* of followers, but the ones she gets are solid and willing to work. And she'll be a bulldog. Won't let go."

"What do you suggest we do now?"

"She's invited me to a banquet at the Sierra Club Wilderness Conference over the weekend. It's a big annual do, I hear. I planned to take my girls waterskiing, but I guess that'll have to wait. I'll go. Sniff around, size things up."

Sibley thought a minute, then picked up the phone. Diercks could tell he was talking to Bob Gerdes' secretary, then Sibley straightened up as he started talking to the boss himself. "Who'd you say you knew in Sierra Club? Some woman? Yes. Diercks is going to a wilderness meeting. I'll tell him to watch out for her." He hung up.

"Look for a woman named Doris Leonard. Gerdes knows her from his law practice. Her husband is an ex-president of the Sierra Club. Gerdes likes her, trusts her."

"Will do—and don't be surprised when an expense voucher shows up for a Sierra Club banquet. Kathy says I can come, but I have to pay my own way!"

8

WILDERNESS MATTERS

KATHY EAGERLY ANTICIPATED THE SIERRA CLUB'S biennial Wilderness Conference of 1963. Wilderness Conferences were bubbling cauldrons of ideas. While the concepts of recreation-centered National Parks were firmly established in the American mind, members saw the further need to set aside wilderness areas where roads, vehicles, logging, mining and development of all kinds were prohibited. How that could be accomplished was argued endlessly. Should such areas be set aside for recreation? For backpackers? As pristine preserves where species could flourish, unhampered by man?

Altogether, the mood at the conference was buoyant. After their Siberian exile during the Eisenhower years, Sierra Club leaders had been welcomed into the Washington offices of members of the Kennedy administration, including Secretary of Interior Stewart Udall. Early in his presidency Kennedy himself had spoken to Congress, requesting passage of a wilderness bill, asking for national seashores such as Point Reyes and calling for establishment of new National Parks.

In any case, the timing was perfect. This was exactly the moment when Kathy needed to contact the most influential conservationists in America so she could explain her quest to wrest the dunes from the clutches of PG&E. And she had laid her plans.

Kathy had already written to Russell and Dorothy Varian. Russell had become enormously wealthy, patenting and manufacturing electronic devices, including microwave amplifiers. Back in San Luis Obispo County, local lore had it that Russell Varian grew up as "a barefoot boy in the dunes." Kathy hoped he had fond memories of his childhood. While he managed his business empire his wife devoted herself to conservation causes, dear to both their hearts. Kathy hoped she might meet with Dorothy, persuade her to influence her husband on behalf of the dunes. Mrs. Varian replied to Kathy's letter, suggesting they meet between seminars.

They met, as agreed. After they laughed a little, reminiscing about High Trips of the past, Kathy got down to business.

"Did you read my letter about the Nipomo Dunes? About PG&E trying to put an atomic power plant there?"

"With great interest," she answered in her kind, low voice. Dorothy was a little shorter than Kathy, but much plumper.

"What do you think?"

"I think you have your work cut out for you. Have you been following Dave Pesonen's efforts at Bodega Bay?"

"Of course. I am learning from him."

Dorothy Varian said little. Kathy searched her face, trying to read her response. "Can you suggest who I should approach to help me? I really don't think we have much time."

Dorothy hesitated for a moment, then looked at the ceiling. "Do you know George Collins?"

"Of course, I've met him." She remembered a balding man, not prepossessing, but intense and cheerful.

"Did you know that he just retired from the National Park Service, and that he, Doris Leonard and I have formed a group called Conservation Associates?"

Kathy's jaw dropped. Here were three people who knew the "frosting" of everyone. George was energetic, brilliantly adept at creating compromise and consensus. Doris had been a stalwart in Sierra Club; her husband was a long-time board member, past president and respected mountain climber. Doris was a dancer, a tennis player, a skier, an indomitable hiker. With access to the

Varian fortune—Kathy had heard it estimated at $75 million—that trio should be able to do anything.

"We will be looking at problem areas that are threatened. Our specialty will be mediating between private industry and conservationists. Our first effort was behind the scenes for the Point Reyes Seashore, which looks pretty secure now."

"The dunes are just as important. Maybe more so."

"We can't promise anything, but we need to know more about your Nipomo dunes. Send us all the information you have, especially about geology."

"I'm no expert. But I'll try." She paused, looked Dorothy Varian straight in the face and pleaded, "Will you help me?"

"I don't know, Kathy. We are being very cautious about how we proceed. We are, after all, a new organization. We don't want to hire a staff, but we expect to be besieged with requests. We will research areas very carefully. After the conference we may have some ideas for you. Meanwhile, you do what you can on the home front."

"I did something. I hope it wasn't wrong. A man named Ken Diercks, from PG&E, has walked with me on the dunes. His job is to influence people in San Luis Obispo County. I invited him to the banquet at the end of the conference. Was that all right?"

"Yes. That is a very good idea." Dorothy Varian seemed to scrutinize Kathy anew, noting the determination in her jaw.

Kathy's immediate problem was to lobby as many members as she could for the dunes, but she faced a formidable rival when it came to getting attention: Rachel Carson. The hot topic that year was *Silent Spring*. The book damning DDT had burst onto the scene in 1962, immediately becoming outrageously popular; suddenly the term "ecology" was on everybody's lips. Against the wishes of the more scientifically inclined members on the board David Brower had invited Carson to the conference. But she declined, probably because the breast cancer that would kill her the following year was already sapping her energy.

Up and down the hotel corridors the battle raged between sessions. People could be overheard saying things like: "She can find leukemia clusters on the flimsiest of evidence."

"But you can't argue with those dead chick embryos."

"If farmers can't use DDT, how will they control flies and mosquitoes?"

"But who cared, until she wrote that book. I tell you it's pure poetry, poetry the common man can relate to."

When she could insert herself between arguments, Kathy buttonholed people she had known from High Trips. They were happy to see bright-eyed Kathy, the little woman whose along-the-trail flirtations, while discreet, had kept the gossip mill crackling. Some of her closest friends had formed a side group who called themselves the "knapsuckers." They prided themselves on backpacking into an area, setting up a campsite a half mile or so off a trail, then leaving the place in such pristine condition that nobody could detect they had been there at all.

"Will you come see the dunes? I'll take you on a hike," she extended the invitation over and over, extracting more than occasional acceptances.

The moment Diercks came through the door Kathleen grabbed his arm and began introducing him to a bewildering variety of people. Diercks, who had a phenomenal ability to learn new names—faces and all—was sorely put to the test. And what people they were!

"Look, over there is Justice William O. Douglas," she said in passing, not wanting to waste the time it would take to wade through the crowd surrounding the Supreme Court Justice who loved the out-of-doors. She preferred to introduce Diercks to members who might impact her crusade. Like a tenacious tug boat she would grab his arm, steer him through throngs of wine-sipping people. He barely had time to establish a conversation when she would nudge him on to the next introduction. Most of the delegates were physicians, lawyers, financiers, bankers, even industrialists; their suits must have been expensive when new. But knotting neckties wasn't nearly as important as knotting ropes so reliably that they could trust their lives to them on a sheer mountain wall. Their vice-grip handshakes differed from the studied grips of politicians. These horny paws reflected the scars and calluses of mountain men. Many women were in attendance, clearly in positions of responsibility and power. They were dressed up, but comfort won over fashion. Most of the attendees looked as though they would like to shuck their city clothes in favor of comfortable Sierra Club garb. In lieu of a campfire, the air hung thick with the scented haze of pipe smoke.

Diercks met Sierra Club President Ed Wayburn, along with his wife Peggy—who wrote many articles for the Bulletin. He met board members Martin Litton and Fred Eissler who, Kathy assured him, were very much against PG&E's plan. Then there was author and activist Wallace Stegner and a short fellow named Will Siri who was planning an Everest expedition. Ansel and Virginia Adams were pointed out. She even managed to get Diercks to David Brower, whose high forehead, chiseled features and shock of hair intensified his fierce expression. Diercks was able to put faces to people he knew only by reputation.

"I don't see many beer bellies or bee-hive hairdos," he quipped to Kathy, when they found their dinner table. Their fellow diners politely quizzed Diercks about Bodega Bay, about PG&E's involvement at Pt. Reyes. He tried to answer as honestly as he could, then expressed surprise at how well informed they were.

When the meal was finished and the lights went down, the Club presented a John Muir Award to Ansel Adams, "In gratitude for his insistence that the great gestures of the earth not be transformed into something less."

When it came time for speeches Carson's editor, Paul Brooks talked about DDT concentrations in fish taken from San Francisco Bay. People glanced at each other uneasily. This brought the problem to their very own beaches. In response Wallace Stegner said: "I certainly cannot speak from scientific knowledge, nor can I speak from wisdom. But I *can* speak from fear. I am running scared..."

Secretary of the Interior Stewart Udall defended the record of the Kennedy administration, decrying "the assumption that man must destroy nature in order to 'conquer' it . . . the assumption that science alone can solve all our problems . . . the assumption that the population explosion is inevitable."

After dinner, Kathy was not yet finished with Diercks. She propelled him toward a slender woman, whose narrow face sparkled with good humor and intelligence. "May I present Doris Leonard," she said. "Doris, this is Ken Diercks, from PG&E. He was asking about you."

"Of course. Bob Gerdes phoned, said I might run into you this evening. How is Bob, still looking at his watch when he's impatient?"

"You know him, all right. Oh yes, and he said to extend his greetings."

"Doris is part of Conservation Associates. I told you about them at dinner."

"Very interesting. I'd like to meet Mrs. Varian and George Collins."

"Would you consider coming to our office, say on Wednesday?"

Kathy hadn't anticipated that things would move this fast. But for her, the Wilderness Conference of 1963 ended on a promising note. Ken Diercks now knew important people, such as those in Conservation Associates. Now she must go home, and start making phone calls. In her euphoria, she was sure that she could convince absolutely everybody she knew that they didn't want an atomic power plant on the Nipomo Dunes.

9

ПОТ QUIET ОП THE HOME FROПT

WHEN THE PRINCESS PHONE next to the Jackson's bed rang at two in the morning Duncan picked it up, then shoved it into Kathy's face. "Here, you answer it."

Sleepily, she lifted it to her ear. "Hello, hello. Who's there?"

A thin voice, clearly disguised said, "What've you got against schools?" and hung up.

"That's strange. Somebody asked what I have against schools. I don't have anything against schools. I wonder what that was all about?"

"Kathy, we've got to talk." Duncan flipped on a bedside lamp.

"But I just got to bed. I had to race down to the depot to catch the mail train. I'm tired."

"If you came to bed at a decent hour, you wouldn't be tired. This isn't the first call in the middle of the night. While you were gone to San Francisco the phone rang two different nights. Nobody said anything, but there was somebody on the line, all right. I don't think it was the old 'if a man answers, hang up' routine. They wanted you, Kathy."

"Why?"

"For a bright woman you can be surprisingly dense. Somebody is trying to shut you up, to make you stop working against PG&E."

"But I have a right . . ."

"You have a right. But is it smart to go against everybody, stick your neck out offending school groups, storekeepers, taxpayers? People are after me all the time, asking if I can't make you stop."

"What do you tell them?"

"The truth. That you have your own ideas."

"That's right, Duncan. I'm truly sorry if my work for the dunes inconveniences you. But I won't stop. I can't."

Duncan turned off the light, sighed and sank into his pillow. After a few moments Kathy moved her hand across to Duncan, indicating her availability. But Duncan rolled over, his back stiffly unyielding.

Other things happened. Somebody would bump into her hard in Safeway; when she turned around they were gone. Or when she entered a restaurant to meet a friend for lunch, conversation would stop, just for a moment, as she entered.

One morning when she answered the phone a woman's voice said, "Maybe you can afford to send your children away to a fancy school in Arizona, but we need better schools here."

If the caller only knew. Kathy had sent two of her teen-aged children—the twins—to Judson School in Arizona to keep them safe from Duncan's wrath. He had never liked them, never saw what Kathleen saw—vulnerable youngsters who needed extra love and protection. Instead, Duncan made Larry a target for the release of his frustrations. On the excuse of a minor infraction he would drag the child behind the pool house, stuff a rag in his mouth and beat him with his belt. Lureen tried to protect her brother, but she was no match for Duncan. In an attempt to rid himself of an annoyance, Duncan agreed to send the twins away to high school.

Well, at least members of her own Santa Lucia group of the Sierra Club were in her corner. That was a comfort.

Lee Wilson was in his element. He had carefully plotted a hike through an area in the Santa Lucia Hills east of San Luis Obispo, and it had gone well. A muscular mountain of a man, an early member of the Santa Lucia Group, he hoped the area would one day be declared the Lopez Wilderness. Much in the way Kathy had adopted the dunes, Wilson had made Lopez Canyon his personal project.

The hike had been strenuous—through rough chaparral, along stream-fed creeks. Trails were little more than game or Jeep paths. But the views of Morro Rock, of Little Falls and Big Falls were all worth the effort. Wilson had been solicitous of the hikers, helpful when people had to squeeze themselves through the occasional barbed wire fence.

Although Wilson rarely came to Kathy's hikes, she often went on his. She always made it a point to join the expeditions of other group leaders. And she was particularly curious about Wilson's willingness, not to say eagerness, to surrender the dunes to PG&E's atomic planners. Wilson was an electrical contractor. The giant utility would be budgeting a fortune for construction expenses. Did Wilson perhaps have an eye out for future business?

It was a delicate issue, not to be tackled head-on. So, following the advice of her friend Lela Burdett, Kathy listened quietly during a riverside lunch break as Wilson expounded on the virtues of Lopez. As Lela said, "Let the man have his day."

On the way home, Kathy was squeezed between Lee and Lela as his old pickup bounced and bumped along a rutted logging road. Kathy felt it was her turn. Wilson was still sounding off about the glories of his beloved canyon.

"Maybe," she ventured "with Kennedy in office the Lopez Wilderness will be authorized." Wrong move! Too late she remembered that she shouldn't have said anything about Kennedy. The burly, opinionated Wilson was a staunch Republican, still arguing after three years for a recount of what he considered to be a crooked vote tally in Illinois. He firmly believed Nixon should be in the White House.

But he merely frowned. "Maybe. Harold Miossi and I have been gathering surveys and statistics. We're thinking about going to Washington."

"First," Kathy said to Wilson, "I really need your help to save the dunes."

Wilson stomped on the gas. "Kathy, don't you understand? San Luis Obispo County has got to have that power plant. It would give us a great tax base, pay half the expenses of our schools. Maybe more."

"But they don't have to put it on the dunes."

"It must be on the dunes. That's the logical place. You don't have a clue about how this kind of thing works. There's not just the power plant to consider, but high voltage lines, access across private property, rights-of-way, a whole slew of matters that I as an electrical contractor am equipped to understand."

And intend to profit from, she wondered? But she checked the impulse to ask. "I realize you're much more knowledgeable than I am, Lee. But are you sure you're looking at the whole picture? At what a power plant and a string of high tension wires would do to the potential of the dunes as a recreational resource?"

Wilson's face was reddening. The road was getting worse and from time to time he had to stop the truck, downshift into its ultra-low gear, then creep slowly in order to avoid straddling a rock. "Aren't you revving the motor too hard?" she asked. There was no way to keep from bumping shoulders when the truck lurched because there was nothing to hang onto.

"Why don't you just stay out of things Kathy? Stick to your knitting. You can't do anything about where that plant goes. The only thing you're doing is making a lot of people mad. Really mad."

Nonplussed, Kathy reached for a straw. "What does Lillian think about this?"

Wilson slammed on the brakes and turned to her in a fury. He looked her straight in the eyes; in his low voice he said very slowly, "Don't you ever even mention my wife's name. Do you hear?" Kathy tried to lean toward Lela, realizing she had once more pushed the wrong button. She knew Lee Wilson loved his wife dearly, was quite aware that Lillian—who proclaimed herself a born-again Christian—loathed her.

Lela had been looking out the window, embarrassed at what had escalated into a full-blown fight. "You two." Lela suddenly broke in. "What are we going to do? If this keeps up, the Santa Lucia group will have to disband. Are you going to let this thing ruin our work, our outings, our friendships?"

Wilson made no answer. In an effort to compromise, Kathy said, "I'll tell you what, Lee. You work for the Lopez Wilderness and let me work for the dunes. Let's agree to stay out of each other's projects. What do you say?"

He still said nothing. Now the only noise was gears shifting, then finally the tires zinging in relief when the truck pulled onto the blessed smoothness of the highway blacktop.

The passengers in the back of the truck had been singing merrily. The first inkling they had of an impasse up front came when Wilson pulled the truck to a stop where they had parked their cars that morning. Wilson slammed his door so hard that the handle fell off.

As Kathy was putting her daypack into her station wagon Wilson came up to her. "You know, don't you, that a lot of those dune buggy people are up in arms. Mean customers. They definitely don't like you horning into their territory. I hear things. . . He paused, then went on in his sinister whisper, "I really don't think you're safe anymore leading hikes out there." He turned abruptly on his heel.

Preparing for bed that night, Kathy thought about Lee's warning, the menace in his voice. To her mind he had a way about him, something that made him seem quite open to dark deeds. Was he threatening her?

For just a flickering moment she wondered if she should abandon the hike announced for the next day. How silly. Of course she should go.

Nonetheless it was with an unshakable sense of dread that she drove toward the dunes the next morning. Her whereabouts were hardly secret. The announcement had appeared in the papers: Mrs. Kathleen Jackson would be leading a hike from Oso Flaco Lake into the Nipomo Dunes. Sometimes the dune buggy people were incredibly rude—and incredibly drunk. But capable of murder? She told herself she was being overly dramatic, but as she drove along she was aware of tears coursing down her cheeks. In private she allowed herself to cry.

"I don't want to die," she sobbed. Once before she had known blinding fear, and she would never forget it.

A long, blazing sunset had been drawing to a close over Teheran. On a hilltop outside the city she was climbing toward a whitewashed, thick-walled rental dwelling. Behind its shuttered windows sat her Persian husband Ali. With a gun.

Before leaving on a buying trip to Bahrein a week before, he had announced that at the slightest breach of Kathy's marital vows he would shoot her down "like a dog." Now he was back, and thanks to a tale-bearing houseboy, was fully aware that during Ali's absence Kathy had not been home to sleep every night. One of the pupils she had been tutoring—they needed money—was a young German, a blond exemplar of a European, everything Ali was not.

How could she have been so stupid? Here she was in a Muslim country, where Western women were suspected, despised and accused of wallowing in loose morals. If Ali shot her—then revealed her infidelity—not only would he get away with it, he might become a national hero.

But she had been so lonely. Ali had changed enormously since their marriage. His conquest achieved, his American trophy bride secured (and his social standing thereby enhanced) he had dropped his engaging facade. On his home ground he stood unmasked as a bully who treated everyone badly. He had never been acknowledged by the respectable, well-positioned family he boasted of at Julius' Castle. Nobody in the Iranian government would give him an audience to explain his aspirations for a national air force. As a businessman he was dishonest, unburdened by conscience; as a lover, mechanical. So when affection was offered from a different source, she melted into Teutonic arms in relief. Not romantic passion, just relief.

She started up the steps, "Kathy, is that you?"

"Yes." She slipped out of her shoes, stepped onto the carpets in the dimly lit room, her shoulders squared, ready to face her fate. She stood before him with her young, pretty, tearstained face. Ali stared at her for a very long time, his lips twitching beneath his mustache, the gun on a table less than a foot away.

"I think," he said finally, "we had better go back to New York."

Kathy gasped. In one glorious, apocalyptic moment she realized he was not going to kill her. "Yes," she said. "That would be a good idea."

Perhaps in his strange, incomprehensible way he really did love her. But it was too late for that. Whatever she had once felt for the dashing aviator had long been expunged by the manipulative tyrant.

She had stayed alive in Teheran and she would stay alive now. To her mild surprise there was no one at the hike assembly point. Not an unprecedented event, but in the light of Lee Wilson's somber forecast a little unnerving. She toyed with the idea of leaving, of taking refuge in surroundings less accessible to mischief-makers.

But a breeze touched her cheek, she heard birds chattering happily in the willows beside the lake, accompanied in the distance by the thunder of the surf. It would be a fine day for a solo exploration of the ever-changing dunes.

After a half hour of aimless strolling a terrible clatter assailed her ears. It was the unmistakable clamor of approaching dune buggies. She quickly looked around but there was not another soul in sight. She was totally alone. In a moment they wheeled into view, three rebuilt VW's, heading like an elongated arrow straight toward her.

Paralyzed with fear, Kathy stood rooted to the spot. Ten yards from contact, the lead vehicle veered abruptly away and the others swerved to follow. As the first buggy roared past, its bearded, heavily tattooed driver waved to Kathy. "Great day, kid!" She remembered him well, a retired sailor with whom she had chatted a few times. As his vehicle retreated she noted that it boasted a bumper sticker, TO HELL WITH SIERRA CLUB.

False alarm. But her panic had been real. And warranted. She was in a tough fight, with more than the crushing strength of PG&E arrayed against her. There was also the dune buggy crowd, especially its roughhouse sector, to reckon with. And beyond that, local business-and-taxes opposition, fanned by the haunting specter of unexpected rebellion from powerful elements in her own Sierra Club Group.

10

UNDER SUPERVISION

THE WEEKLY MEETINGS OF THE SUPERVISORS of San Luis Obispo County tended to be relaxed, neighborly, almost jovial. Few citizens bothered to attend. This one was different. With the PG&E power plant on the agenda for April 6, 1964, feelings were running hot and heavy. Twenty minutes before the ten o'clock gavel, all the good seats were taken. Teetering on her spike heels a secretary, topped by a jet-black bee-hive hairdo, bustled along the long table atop a platform, doling out stacks of mimeographed copies for each supervisor.

Despite the early Monday morning hour, Kathy had arrived ahead of time. Scheduled to deliver what might be a definitive pleading for the dunes, she had found herself a bit distracted of late; along with much of the rest of the country, she was still reeling from the murder of John F. Kennedy the previous November. As if that weren't enough, she had recently discovered that the Collier Corporation, a local petroleum refinery, was planning to erect a coke conveyor belt that would scar the dunes from the shore across to the Southern Pacific railroad.

But she could not let herself lose her focus on her first priority—the atomic energy plant. With the help of Lela Burdett, the monthly hikes planned to follow the entire coastline of San Luis Obispo County had proved very popular. They drew scores of participants who were new to Sierra Club outings; to each group, during lunch breaks, she had voiced passionate concern over the threat to the dunes, rallying a small army of followers who dutifully volunteered to campaign. But without a leader the army would fade away. That responsibility was hers.

The five supervisors were trickling in, taking their places on a raised dais, facing the audience.

Most of the audience was composed of the power elite of San Luis Obispo County; she knew many of them. Seated among the local bigwigs, the object of elaborate attention, was Ken Diercks who waved to her; she could read nothing in his glance. She noted that State Senator Vern Sturgeon was at his side—gladding the hands around him. The tall, slender, capable senator was in the dairy business; he was well thought of, popular and more accessible than many politicians. Another local businessman, Mike Hermrick, was grinning confidently as though this hearing were merely a formality before ground was broken on the dunes.

Kathy knew she was heavily out-gunned. County Supervisors Lyle Carpenter and Fred Kimball—although ostensibly there to *hear* arguments, had voiced their enthusiasm about PG&E on frequent occasions. There were reporters there, too, not only from the *Telegram-Tribune* but also from Paso Robles and even Santa Maria.

Those who had asked to speak in favor of the project seemed to have come straight out of Ken Diercks' playbook. The first was Bill Troxall from the Chamber of Commerce who stood up and advanced to the speaker's podium brandishing sheets of paper. The Chamber, he declared, with the backing of its South County colleagues and the Oceano Improvement Association, was petitioning Governor Edmund G. Brown to retain the industrial-development status of the dunes, claiming their smog-free winds would shelter residential areas. The new plant would provide one-third of the county's tax, a figure that would be supplemented by the Collier Corporation's $3.5 million conveyor belt.

"The people in the south county are the taxpayers and are paying the bills," said Troxall. "If we lose these ventures to the Sierra Club, we will lose the entire area to industry or manufacturing ventures. Besides, the area proposed for the plant is of doubtful recreational and scenic value."

Kathy and Lela Burdett exchanged glances, shaking their heads in disbelief.

Charles Anders, who introduced himself as president of the Oceano Improvement Association, stood up next: "Of a $150 million bond issue passed last year by the legislature for state beaches and parks, only $22 million was designated for land purchase. With the Nipomo Dunes so far down the priority list, it will be untold years before the state has money available to purchase this wasteland."

Kathy twitched at the word *wasteland*.

Mike Hermick praised the notion that PG&E was exploring the idea of combining an atomic power plant with a facility that would convert seawater to fresh water. Speaker after speaker extolled the virtues of additional taxes—declaring the money would cure welfare by putting people onto payrolls.

Finally, it was Kathy's turn to speak. A genial buzz of conversation was drifting through the audience. Kathy stood up, crossed the room to the podium. The chairman had to gavel the audience to silence. "You had your say, gentlemen. Please be polite enough to listen to Mrs. Jackson."

Discreetly attired in suit, hat, gloves and purse—a proper society matron—she was aware that some people looked upon the practical Sierra Club trail khakis as little more than a boy-scoutish affectation. She was careful to present herself to the government and business community, not as a wild-eyed long-haired mountain woman, but as one of their own, the wife of the county's Republican Party chairman. Lela, along with an sizable contingent of Sierra Club regulars and new recruits, fastened attention on their champion.

Less reassuring was the bulky presence of Lee Wilson whispering to his cronies a few feet away, frowning his disapproval.

The old throb came up the back of her throat, but she suppressed it, along with the tears just behind it. She felt as shaky as though she were still in high school, getting ready to give her speech for the Barry Oratory Cup. Now the contest was for real, and the stakes were very high. These might be the most important words she would ever speak.

"There was once a wonderful place. A magical place. The twin canyon to Yosemite, it was called the Hetch-Hetchy Canyon and it was threatened. The great mining attorney Will Colby said: 'Hetch-Hetchy is an immortal canyon, filled with the music of waterfalls, laced with green forests, a second Yosemite. And we are going to *need* a second Yosemite someday for the thousands, perhaps millions, who will come. We of the Sierra Club are not against water for the city of San Francisco; we are not against dams. We are for dams—in the proper location.'

"Well—the battle of Hetch-Hetchy was lost by the Sierra Club. But what prophetic words were those that Will Colby spoke in 1909! A second Yosemite is needed today. The city of San Francisco gets water elsewhere, anyway. The valley of Hetch-Hetchy would be a rich scenic and spiritual resource, and a richer economic gain as a tourist mecca than as it is, a barren and disheartening reservoir, with an ugly fluctuating waterline, where dead stumps of giant trees still rise when the water is low, to haunt anyone who goes there—and few people do go to this gaunt and unattractive place. A valley lost. And income lost."

Some in the audience looked at their feet, unable to make eye-contact with the speaker. Others looked away. But all were listening. For just a moment she wondered if she had infiltrated their collective consciences.

"This is exactly what the Sierra Club is saying now in San Luis Obispo County about the lovely Nipomo Dunes with their industrial zoning.

"Industry does not belong in this area that is uniquely scenic with its wind-sculptured white sands and its green flowering glades, an area which is rich scientifically, which offers historic interest, and which has the potential of a wider variety of recreation than any other single state park and recreation area in the entire state of California. We in the Sierra Club are not against industry. We are not against power plants, piers, conveyors and factories. We like a comfortable tax base. We approve of industry—in the proper location.

"The real significance of recreation and scenery is a cultural matter. It is far more than hunting, fishing, hiking, camping or beach sports; it has to do with the human spirit. And what we are trying to conserve is not scenery and recreation as much as the human spirit itself."

When she sat down there was no applause for just a moment. Then Ken Diercks and Vern Sturgeon started to clap. And the audience followed their example, hesitantly at first, then with gathering warmth.

"Kathy, you do have a way with words. Are you sure you're not thinking about running for office?" said Senator Sturgeon as he approached her. Diercks was at his side, nodding his agreement.

The senator looked at her squarely, "Did you mean that? That you aren't against power plants?"

"Certainly. Not at all."

He turned to his companion, "You ask her, Ken."

"We want you to come with us to visit the plant at Humboldt Bay. We think you would be interested in learning more about atomic technology."

When Kathleen was surprised, she often let her jaw drop—literally. On this occasion she faced the men, mouth open, then remembering—touched her finger to her chin to close her mouth.

"Well, I must think about that. Who else would go?"

"Whoever you want," said Diercks. "Vern wants to take a look at it."

As she drove home, Kathy thought about the day. It didn't feel as though she was gaining any ground in her crusade, but she wasn't losing any, either. She was sure her words had genuinely touched those present, made them see that her eternal verities went beyond theirs. Now, about this Humboldt thing. Should she go? She must ask Fred Eissler. He was a good friend, a member of the board of directors of the Sierra Club, who had let it be known that he was totally opposed to PG&E's presence on the dunes.

Fred Eissler was an English teacher. He opposed nuclear energy in any form, and had sent Kathy a steady stream of articles and literature disputing what were generally still perceived to be its promise. Kathy had read all of it, tried hard to understand the scientific treatises, and had sent copies along to Ken Diercks.

She called him. "Eissler here."

"Fred, this is Kathy Jackson. I want your opinion about something. Vern Sturgeon and Ken Diercks, from PG&E, have asked me to go up to Humboldt Bay to see the atomic power plant they have up there. They said I could bring people with me. Will you go?"

"Absolutely not. But Kathleen Jackson, don't you go, either. If you accept this invitation you will be snowed, and in their nuclear bag. You will never be an effective spokesman again. I am against atomic power anywhere, for any reason, for anyone. I don't want any plants to be built—ever."

But, in a rare twist, it was Duncan's opinion that won the day. He argued that in the name of fairness, she should accept the invitation. And he offered to accompany her.

FEELING HUMBOLDT

THE PILOT OF THE TWIN-ENGINE AIRPLANE dipped its starboard wing so his passengers could view the Humboldt Nuclear Power Plant from the air. Kathy's first thought was how lovely the beach would look without the intrusion of the steaming stacks. Ken Diercks had driven Kathy, Duncan and Vern Sturgeon to San Francisco. There, they climbed aboard the executive aircraft PG&E had chartered for the purpose of taking the small party to see the plant at Humboldt Bay, a few miles south of Eureka.

"Is that smoke coming out of the stack?" she asked.

"No," Diercks assured her. "Excess steam—just vapor. Like at Morro Bay," he said, referring to an existing fossil fuel plant that had been built in 1951 in San Luis Obispo County with little resistance—but was thought by most people to stand in ugly contrast to the bay's famous rock. Bill Nutting, another PG&E executive, was pointing out various features to Diercks.

"It doesn't look as big as the plant in Morro Bay," Kathy said, over the noise of the engines.

"Our next plant will be at least ten times this size," responded Diercks.

A van took them from the local air strip to the plant. They drove along a barbed wire fence draped with dire warnings: No Trespassing, KEEP OUT: RADIOACTIVITY, Restricted to Authorized Personnel Only. At a security gate a guard, recognizing a familiar driver, waved them through without so much as a glance into the back seat.

The party was ushered into an anteroom where each member was issued all-white overalls with a hood to go over their hair—along with booties that slipped over their shoes. Kathy wasn't sure whether she looked like a medical technician or somebody from outer space. Then they were handed badges, and told to pin them to their overalls. "This badge registers the level of radiation, we'll keep an eye on it."

"My, it must be dangerous in there," she said.

"Don't worry, we've never had a problem yet." Their businesslike guide, who turned out to be the plant manager, assured her: "We ask you to put on the costume partly to protect you, but just as much to maintain our clean room. Dust and foreign material might affect the controls."

"I'm glad we don't have to wear outfits like this to milk cows," joked Sturgeon, referring to his dairy farms. "They'd be so scared they couldn't give milk."

Kathy liked the manager, he reminded her of Sierra Club members who were rugged, competent, assured. The tour began when he led them into a large room, fairly dimly lit, where banks of control panels were studded with blinking lights, switches, knobs, and control levers. On the walls were dozens of gauges, most of which looked like clocks with arrows instead of hands; each seemed to have a patch of red, presumably indicating a danger point.

The manager launched a mini-lecture. "The Humboldt facility is a boiling water reactor. The reactor was built to our specifications by General Electric. Compared to the power plants that will come after this, ours is relatively small, merely 63 megawatts. We envision plants that will be many times this size.

"Please look at this chart," he pointed to a detailed schematic on the wall then traced its components with his finger. "It isn't very complicated, really. Power is produced by boiling water to make steam—no different really than the principle that operates a steam locomotive on a train."

Except that, thought Kathy to herself, good old coal never blew up Hiroshima or Nagasaki.

"That chart is the same as this flow schematic." He turned to an electric console that looked something like the chart. "Note that there are sensors connected to warning lights that immediately alert us when and where there is trouble."

She tried to follow the engineer's explanation—about how water was heated in the nuclear reactor core to approximately 570 degrees, Fahrenheit, to make steam at 1,000 pounds per square inch. About how the heat was generated by the reactor core, about how the heated water then gave up its heat in a heat exchanger to a separate system of water which became steam. How the steam was directed to drive a turbine which finally produced electricity by driving the generator. How the heated water was then chilled in the cooling system. About turbines, generators, transformers. How a lot of cold water was needed to operate the plant safely and efficiently.

Duncan seemed to be getting it, fortunately, but a glance in the direction of Diercks indicated he wasn't doing much better than she was. She looked around the control room. A dozen or so men were methodically checking the gauges and lights, some carried clip boards. They smiled at the party of visitors, then turned to their notations. To Kathy, who relished nothing as much as the outdoors, it seemed that being locked in this ultra-sanitized room must amount to hours and hours of claustrophobia . . . a very boring way to live.

One lanky young fellow wearing safety goggles was introduced as the Safety Engineer. He nodded pleasantly, explained that nobody who worked there was the least bit worried about safety, "I feel safer here than I do at home in bed at night."

Then the party proceeded to the turbine-generator room. It was a vast, fairly empty hall, with an overhead crane fixed on tracks so it could be moved to lift heavy machinery when necessary. A loud but low hum constituted the only evidence that at that very moment electricity was being generated to be sent all over Northern California. She could feel a faint vibration, but her overall impression was that there wasn't much to see. She knew the turbines were spinning, but they were totally hidden under white-domed structures.

Kathy could not help being impressed. Everything seemed so smooth, scientific, under control. But then she thought about Fred Eissler's warning and wondered what these fellows, so slick and competent, *weren't* telling her. And she felt lost because she really didn't even know what to ask.

They were hosted at a nearby restaurant for lunch; Kathy offered to pay for her own meal, but was assured that the company ran a tab.

Diercks guided the conversation. "PG&E first considered the possibilities of atomic energy in 1955. Norm Sutherland, who became president then, was very interested. This plant was first proposed in 1957. As you know, Washington is anxious to implement peacetime uses of atomic energy. This was one of the first nuclear power plants ever built.

"Of course, Bodega Bay has made us aware that finding a site for such a plant is more complicated than we anticipated."

"Is this site free from earthquake faults?" asked Kathy.

"When it was built, that was not a major consideration. However, since then the site has been surveyed and yes, there are a few concerns. But I'm glad to tell you that there isn't a major fault here . . ."

"Not like the San Andreas," quipped Kathy, referring to the fact that PG&E discovered, too late, that the site of the proposed plant at Bodega Bay would sit almost squarely on the San Andreas fault. The project had to be abandoned.

"We're paying a lot more attention now to our geologists," continued Diercks. "Sutherland developed a list of what he called Super Sites, places he believed would be ideal for atomic plants. I don't have to tell you that the gas-fired plants at Moss Landing near Monterey and Morro Bay have come in for a lot of criticism because they impact scenic areas. Let's face it, the California Coast is almost all scenic."

"Are the Nipomo Dunes one of the Super Sites?" asked Kathleen.

"Yes, one of them," admitted Diercks.

Kathy frowned. She had not known that. There was a distinct pause in the conversation. But Duncan had something on his mind, "Has this plant amortized PG&E's investment?"

Kathy thought that was a very good question.

"Well, of course this plant is experimental. So it's not really fair to say—but I'll try to get you some figures," promised Diercks. Kathy could tell that Duncan had hit a sore point. But she had learned that when Diercks said he would produce facts and figures, he meant it.

"Does Humboldt County receive much in the way of taxes from this plant?" asked Vern Sturgeon.

"Well, they don't turn them down," joked the manager. "It isn't a lot, but it's better than a poke in the eye." Everyone laughed.

Diercks added, "The economic impact of a plant here is minor compared to what it would do for San Luis Obispo County."

The conversation turned briefly to fishing. Taking advantage of the distraction, Kathy asked Diercks. "Do you understand all of this?"

"No, I have to say I don't. You know, Kathy, there are different kinds of engineers. Most of them know the technical stuff. I guess you could call me a political engineer."

"And am I the raw material?" He didn't argue the point.

As dessert was served, the plant manager asked. "Now, are there any more questions?"

"Just one," said Kathy. "What do you do with the radioactive fuel when you're done with it?"

His answer was as swift as it was troubling. "We don't know yet, but we think that in a couple of years that will be answered. Until then, we'll just store it right here."

On the return flight, as the airplane droned its way south, Kathy noted that the young man who had been introduced as the

Safety Engineer had come aboard, too, hitching a ride to San Francisco.

"Would it be all right if I talk to him?" she asked Diercks.

He hesitated for a moment, then said: "Of course."

She squeezed sideways down the narrow aisle and slipped into the seat next to the engineer. He was gazing out the window, fascinated by the forests and streams below, but turned and smiled.

"My, but you certainly have a responsible job," she said pleasantly. "What did you say your title was?"

"Chief Safety Engineer."

"I'll bet PG&E required a lot of special training for that."

"Of course."

"Did you need a graduate degree in physics?"

"I have a degree from Cal Poly," he said with pride. "In air conditioning."

Kathy was appalled and alarmed. Her doubts about the world of technology were reinforced.

When they returned to San Francisco, Vern Sturgeon traveled on to his office in Sacramento. It was night when they drove south from San Francisco. Duncan dozed in the back seat while Kathy chatted with Diercks. Over the course of their encounters, she had come to respect Ken Diercks' Irish enthusiasm, and his German integrity. When Ken said something, she could be assured that he was telling the truth, unlike some members of her own Sierra Club.

"Let me ask you something, Kathy."

"Anything."

"You've said that the Sierra Club has no objections to atomic power plants. Where would *you* put one, if you could have your way?"

Later, what she said next would come back to haunt her. "Why, there are many little slot canyons along the coast. They're pretty enough, filled with oaks, but there are lots of them. They're not unique, like the dunes. You should look up north, along Avila Bay."

The next day, after she returned to Paso Robles, Kathy called Fred Eissler to report on her trip. There was silence at the other end of the phone as she described her adventure.

After her spiel, the silence continued until she wasn't sure he was still there. Then he said slowly, firmly, "Well, you've been snowed. I can see that, and I knew that would happen, and I'm not going to have anything to do with your carryings-on with Pacific Gas and Electric Company."

"Well, Fred, I have come to a very difficult decision and that is that I do not have physics in my college training. I do not have the scientific background for understanding the hazards of nuclear waste, the threats of nuclear power, but I believe that this campaign can be about things that *are* there and that I *do* know that I *can* recognize. I am going to work on the scientific values and beauty of the Nipomo Dunes. I am going to do my best to get to know the people in PG&E, and I want them to know Sierra Club people, and I am going to suggest that all of us try to *educate* PG&E to change their plans and leave the dunes of San Luis Obispo County alone; eventually, hopefully, put it up for state park acquisition to be added to the Pismo-to-Point Sal complex. This has been in the minds of several directors of parks and recreation whom I have known, and this is what I plan to do."

Eissler responded, curtly. "You will fail. Education won't work with PG&E, and I will continue to alert people to the hazards of having nuclear power anywhere around."

Kathleen Goddard was born to William Russell Goddard and Nellie Sartoris Carr Goddard, on July 2, 1907 in Sacramento, California.

Kathy as an infant; Little Kathy grew up in Santa Barbara where she participated in Camp Fire Girls and wrote poems and stories for the newspaper.

A couple of weeks after Kathy Goddard graduated from Santa Barbara High School in 1925, an earthquake shook the city to its foundations. She went to work helping librarians sort books that had been jumbled by the temblor.

Kathy probably posed this picture, in 1929, to show her parents what her life
was like in India. Ambitious to be a writer, she works at her typewriter. Her
husband, Ali Shiraz reads a newspaper. Two servants are in attendance.

For Kathy, visits to temples in Rangoon or
India were adventures into a glorious past.
Ali was less interested; history did not inter-
est him as much as commerce.

Kathy joined a tennis club where most of the members were the half-caste descendants of the English Raj, occupiers of India. She sits on the bench, third from the left. 1929.

For a while in New York, Kathy worked for a glamour photographer who posed her for this picture in 1931. But she soon found more interesting work at the NBC stenographer pool. There she mastered the world of public relations.

Kathy met her second husband—the
wealthy Duncan Jackson—when she
sat next to him on a train after visiting her parents in Santa Barbara.

Kathy Jackson was a proper young society matron
in Santa Barbara in the 1940s. But she was more
comfortable in Sierra Club garb.

The Jacksons' adopted children on their bikes, 1949. Before she
joined the Sierra Club, Kathy Jackson was very active in issues
surrounding adoption.

In line with Kathy's new interest in the Sierra Club, the Jackson children were portrayed wearing backpacks on the family's 1951 Christmas greeting. From left to right: Gay, Carol, Michael, Lureen, Larry, Beatrice Delgado, Kathleen and Duncan. Beatrice's widowed mother, who was ill with tuberculosis, declined to allow the Jacksons to adopt Beatrice. The Jacksons treated her as a daughter and appreciated her help with the younger children.

Duncan and Kathy bought Janney House when they moved from Santa Barbara to Paso Robles. During World War II, it had been converted into a warren of small apartments to house the families of soldiers at nearby Camp Roberts. The Jacksons remodeled it extensively, keeping its Victorian character in the front; in the back they installed a large swimming pool where their large family, and friends, enjoyed many pool parties.

On a Sierra Club High Trip, August, 1951, getting ready to start the day's hike. From the left, Roberta Colaw Moran, Hope Harvey MacIntyre, Kathy Jackson, Bob Cutter, Audrey Pass Austin, Brad Breyman (just his hat showing), Marian Beck Daughtry, Jean Ackerman Maderis, Fritz Schnider.

Bob Cutter, Cutter Laboratories, gives a fishing lesson to Kathy and Hope Harvey, 1951.

Courtesy of Roberta Moran

In the Sierras, a bridge is where you find it. Kathy balances her camera on the way to safety across a stream at McGee Lakes, 1951.

Courtesy of Roberta Moran

Kathy with Tom Jukes, founder of the Sierra Club's Atlantic Chapter, in King's Canyon National Park near Sawmill Pass, August, 1952.

Courtesy of Roberta Moran

Kathy with Jerry Fisher, a Sierra Club member from Hawaii, August, 1952.

Two views of the Dunes that Kathleen fought so long and hard to preserve.

At first, Kathleen wasn't sure what to make of Ken Diercks, PG&E's representative—an astute executive who had worked his way up through the ranks of the company's bureaucracy.

When Kathy made a six-week trek into the Golden Trout area of the Sierras in the summer of 1966 her only companion was a burro named Sambo. Taken at Henry Brown's Fish Camp on the Kern River.

Kathleen and Gaylord,
about 1980.

When she met Gaylord Jones, Kathleen at last discovered a soulmate.
They are pictured on the dunes in their standard dune outfits, 1970s.

When Kathleen led hikes she frequently initi-
ated people into the society of "dunites." They
were told to stand at the top of a dune, take a
very deep breath, then run down screaming
at the tops of their lungs. They were charged
to reach the bottom in one breath, 1987.

An attentive group takes in Kathleen's accumulated wisdom of dune lore, 1988.

On April 8, 1995, Kathleen gathered many of her friends to dedicate a monument on Coreopsis Hill, near Oso Flaco Lake. Dedicated to the family of Joseph Enos, the plaque celebrated the descendents of Joseph Enos who immigrated from the Azore Islands in 1894. Kathleen devised the inscription, with mention of the appreciation she and her late husband Gaylord Jones had for the magnificent rare species of flowers that grow in that location. Volunteers have planted and watered young oak trees nearby.

Kathleen chats with an admirer at the opening of the Dune Discovery Center, the temporary educational facility opened in Guadalupe in 1996. It was supplanted when the Dune Center opened in 2000.

Courtesy of Bill Denneen

Leading a hike to the Dune Monument on Coreopsis Hill on the occasion of her ninetieth birthday, July 3, 1997, Kathleen paused with two of her faithful followers, Bill Denneen and Jack Beigle.

Courtesy of Virginia Cornell

In her later years, near her home on Halcyon Road in Arroyo Grande, friends installed a bench so Kathleen would have a place to rest on her daily walk. Her sentiments are as "advertised."

12

IT IS MAGNIFICENT!

THROUGH THE AUTUMN, ALTHOUGH KATHY kept looking for a breakthrough on the dunes, interest in them was confined mainly to an announcement that movie stars were coming to town. A film crew from Hollywood would be shooting scenes at the beach for a movie to be called "The Great Race." Residents were agog with the knowledge that such stars as Jack Lemmon, Tony Curtis and Natalie Wood might be checking into the Tides Motel in Pismo Beach. On the Oceano portion of the dunes, race car drivers would "suffer" the rigors of crossing a desert.

Such nonsense didn't occupy Kathy much. When she contacted the people in Conservation Associates their answers were evasive, "We're working on it, Kathy. We should have more news before long."

When after several weeks Doris Leonard finally called, her cheerful voice held an extra note of enthusiasm, "Kathy, we have some good news for you."

"Wonderful, what is it?"

"Dorothy Varian and I went to Boulder, Colorado to learn more about your dunes."

"Boulder, Colorado? Are there sand dunes there?"

"No, but a professor of geology at the University of Colorado named William S. Cooper . . ."

"Cooper. Oh yes, I met him a few times on the dunes."

"Well, he is in the process of writing a monograph for the

Geological Society of America about the dunes. To make a complicated geological explanation simple, he says that their cross-layer-
ing is unique. He knows of no other formation like it in the whole
world."

"Unique? Unique? Isn't that what I always said?"

"Yes, and you were right."

"I've been talking to Will Siri," Doris said, referring to the new
president of the Sierra Club. "I urged him to visit the dunes, to
assess the situation for himself."

Kathy allowed herself to dance a jubilant jig, then quickly got
to work planning the event. This was it! The Sierra Club was going
to give her its blessing.

First, the Club gave Kathy permission to release its position to
the press. On November 19, 1964, an article appeared on the first
page of the *San Luis Obispo Telegram-Tribune*:

Sierra Club spells out stand

The Sierra Club favors development of nuclear
power facilities in California, but urges careful consideration of site location to preserve scenic natural
resources, such as the Nipomo Dunes.

The position of the Sierra Club was spelled out
today by Mrs. Kathleen Jackson, president of the
Santa Lucia Group of the Sierra Club, in connection
with the proposed PG&E nuclear power plant in southern San Luis Obispo County. The site is in the vicinity
of the Nipomo Dunes.

Mrs. Jackson said it is the policy of the Sierra Club
to obtain its objectives through negotiation rather
than by collision.

"I am confident," she said, "that by continuing our
present talks between conservation organization representatives, PG&E and the State Department of Parks
and Recreation we will eventually resolve the Nipomo
Dunes issue."

The article went on to declare that the club's board of directors would meet on Saturday, December 12 to discuss the Nipomo Dunes.

Kathleen's release did not go unnoticed. The next day William Troxell, president of the Pismo Beach Chamber of Commerce, spoke to that group. As the newspaper reported, he flatly declared he was against any and all defenders of the dunes:

South County wants plant

San Luis Obispo County must be ready to move with nuclear speed and atomic-age thinking if it is to assure location of a multi-million-dollar Pacific Gas & Electric Co. power plant on the Nipomo Mesa.

We must organize, and remain organized, to do war with any group which might now or later oppose location of the PG&E power plant," Troxall said.

Troxall argued that the plant might eventually mean $50 million worth of evaluation to be added to the county tax rolls—an increase of one-third. He noted that PG&E had given its assurance that the plant would be designed with the preservation of the dunes' natural beauty in mind.

From San Francisco came a measured response. Will Siri would visit the dunes in person, January 15, 1965.

Kathleen immediately alerted the local media. Newspapers from as far away as Santa Maria and Santa Barbara were interested. After all, Dr. Siri—a biophysicist from the University of California at Berkeley—was a national figure. He had just returned from an expedition up the west ridge of Mt. Everest where, in addition to his legendary mountain climbing expertise he was in charge of keeping records of the climbers' blood chemistry.

Early in the morning on the big day a television/radio station in Santa Maria called to ask Kathy why they hadn't been invited.

"I didn't think your equipment could go out there."

The station manager replied, "If the story is big enough, we'll find the equipment. We've found a truck with big balloon tires that will haul everything."

"Wonderful," she shouted, "you're invited!"

The day dawned bright and the sun never retreated. The blue, blue sky was laced with frilly white clouds. The dunes dazzled, seemingly reflecting billions of tiny gems. Flowers seemed to bloom on cue.

Trailed by panting reporters, the Sierra Club hikers strode forth from Oso Flaco Lake to meet the more sedentary representatives from PG&E and local government who were being ferried to the agreed-upon spot by members of the Pismo Dune Riders. Siri was a small man, whose wiry form was as comfortable scrambling up the side of a mountain as it was in the classroom. Marching at a brisk pace, Bernard and Lela Burdett and other members followed Kathy. She deliberately kept up a challenging pace, because she didn't want her guest of honor to pause until she had reached the perfect spot. So lively was her stride that at one point Will Siri commented to a reporter, "I sometimes thought it was easier climbing Mount Everest." When they had scrambled to the top of the first high ridge, a place where the panorama of dunes, bay, sea and sky was particularly vast, she stopped and said, "Look."

Will Siri stopped in his tracks, breathing heavily. His eyes roamed across the shimmering sand, out to the sea. To the north, south, all along the beach. His lungs filled with pure ocean air. Then he threw out his arms wide, "I didn't know it looked like this. It is magnificent!"

At long last, thought Kathy, the Sierra Club sees this wonderful place the way I do.

As luck would have it, on the first of January Kathy had surrendered her office as chairman of the Santa Lucia Group to—Lee Wilson. He could hardly insult the president of the national Sierra Club by boycotting the occasion, but it is noteworthy that in surviving pictures, his is the only unsmiling face.

As for Kathy, no photographer that day caught her without a grin as wide as the brim on her hat.

When they rendezvoused with the men from PG&E at the

appointed spot on their land, Siri exclaimed, "This is my first trip here. This is California's most magnificent stretch of coastline."

To which Diercks admitted, "It's scenic, all right," adding that he had visited the area about eighteen times. Kathy raised an eyebrow. Not *to* the dunes, she thought to herself, but to organize against them, perhaps. Diercks introduced Hal Stroube, PG&E's nuclear energy expert from San Francisco, who handled the few technical questions that were raised.

Bill Glines, the staff writer for the *San Luis Obispo Telegram-Tribune* contrasted the pipe-smoking Siri with the cigarette-puffing Diercks.

Siri's declared intention was to inspect the area with a future state park in mind. Because of time considerations, the party piled onto dune buggies and trucks, which hastened them south to inspect the Union Oil facility by the Santa Maria River. Then it was back to Oceano for lunch at Carl's Spanish Seas restaurant.

On the surface, harmony drove the rhythm of the day. At the Spanish Seas, representatives of the two organizations were anxious to sound amicable.

Diercks explained that PG&E had searched up and down the coast for a nuclear energy plant site. "This is it. I can think of nothing in our planning that is not generally compatible with Sierra Club aims. PG&E has no argument with Sierra Club. After all, we have been negotiating about this for two years."

In a general mood of agreement, Siri said: "The Sierra Club wants to see a substantial part of the dunes preserved. The public must have access to it. There are competitive interests involved, PG&E's and the Sierra Club's. I'd say that we are going about this in a rational, reasonable manner."

"There will be plenty of access to the dunes," said Diercks. "We will fence off only that area where the plant is built. The rest of the eleven hundred acres will be left open."

It was then that Siri shot back, "That five hundred feet from the ocean you've planned isn't enough."

"We own the property," Diercks replied firmly. "This is part of our contract with the county. We will locate the plant where it is best for everyone concerned. The economics are important. After all, PG&E is largely owned by California investors. Power users must be considered."

Beneath the amicable words, serious differences were lurking.

The evening meeting at the Golden Tee restaurant in Morro Bay, less political, was a sell-out. Siri showed slides about his climb up Mt. Everest. To Kathy's satisfaction, the event drew more people who might help work for the dunes.

The next day, as she drove Will Siri to the airport, Kathy had some serious questions. "That was a very pleasant day yesterday, but you and Ken Diercks sounded as though you will be putting the power plant right there on the dunes. That's not what I want."

"I know, Kathy, but it was necessary to make some show of public agreement."

"What will the Sierra Club be doing? Will they support the dunes? Keep PG&E out?"

"I can't tell you right now. But we are very interested in their preservation."

"How does the *board* feel about it?"

"For the most part, they agree with you. But that isn't unanimous."

"What about David Brower?" she asked.

Siri did not reply. His shrug made her understand that Brower was a wild card in this negotiation.

As they pulled into the airport Siri said, "Kathy, there is one more thing. And it is very important."

"Yes?"

"Things are very delicate right now. When you go to public meetings, make it clear you are speaking as an individual, and not for the Club."

"Why?"

"Because anything that is said on behalf of the Club must be sanctioned from San Francisco. Surely you understand that."

"Yes," she said, although she felt like a small child who had been disciplined. "That goes for written statements as well. If you write a letter to the paper, you can pass it by somebody for approval. All right?"

13

WE CANNOT COMPROMISE

THERE WERE TIMES WHEN THE BEACHES and dunes seized public attention— in a very big way. On the weekend following Siri's visit, January 16-17, 1965, tides of close to minus two feet uncovered vast stretches of the tidal bed. A horde estimated at 143,000 people descended on the beaches to dig for succulent Pismo clams. Like a mighty convoy they advanced, mostly in private automobiles, armed with digging forks and pails. By Sunday evening the excitement had taken a terrible toll: thirty temporarily lost children, fifty-two persons treated for clam fork wounds to their feet, twenty citations for undersized or over-the-limit clams. Worst of all, in their exertion two men suffered heart attacks and died on the beach. It was estimated that over a million clams were taken.

As Kathy read about the unruly crowd she shook her head. The Pismo clams, she knew, would soon be endangered. Perhaps she could return to that problem later. For now she had to look at a bigger picture.

It was clear that pro-plant factions were organizing. The day of Will Siri's visit a poignant letter from Larue Lee of Oceano appeared in the San Luis Obispo paper:

> . . . Perhaps I have a bit of a selfish motive because my husband has had a hand in building most of these plants. . . . And due to the fact there is not one of these plants in the building process in this area at this time,

> particularly the PG&E plant on the Nipomo Mesa, we
> know only too well . . . what the greater tragedy of no
> work to be found to buy even necessities actually
> means. We have many friends who are in the same
> spot we are. Some have lost homes and cars and gone
> so far into debt it will take years to get on top again.
> The men go any place there is a chance of a little work
> to be had. . . . For the last few days my own husband
> has been getting out of bed about 4 a.m. to go and
> check on various places he just might be able to go to
> work. Ever since last May he has been going to a job
> in Los Angeles and paying for room and board, to say
> nothing of extra gas for his weekend trips home, so he
> could bring home at least part of a pay check to keep
> our home which we bought here five years ago.

The economy would constitute the opposition's most persuasive argument. Kathy noted that on February 9 the superintendent of schools for the Arroyo Grande district had warned his trustees that a land trade could be in the offing. The subtext of his announcement was that the plant might go elsewhere—perhaps to Santa Barbara County, considered to be far wealthier than its northern neighbor. But the next day, from San Francisco PG&E's Hal Stroube pronounced it "nothing but a rumor."

In another letter to the editor Chester D. Porter, Arroyo Grande, wrote, "I wonder if the Sierra Club would stand ready to compensate San Luis Obispo County and the south county area for the loss of a community asset? . . . an unbroken panorama of sea, sky and sand dunes is indeed small comfort and consolation to those whose eyes and minds are dimmed by the economic squeeze of reduced income and higher taxes."

Senator Vernon Sturgeon felt called upon to reiterate his support for the Nipomo Dunes site. He poured fuel on the fire when he stated, "About 99 1/2 % of the public is in favor of the plant. The half percent that doesn't favor it are conservationists." He did, however, state that he would prefer the plant be 5,000 feet from the ocean, but said that 1,700 would be acceptable.

In mid-February the eloquent conservationist Ian McMillan of
Shandon plunged into the fray:

Conservation strength needed

To the editor:

It has been interesting to note your reports on the
panic that developed over the threatened "loss" of a
projected power plant in this county. Appearing to be
the most critically affected by this panic was Senator
Sturgeon. His proposition that "the half per cent who
don't favor it are conservationists," while obviously an
outburst of emotion, couldn't have been more signifi-
cant of what is lacking in this county far more than a
multi-million dollar power development.

It is a strange paradox that here in San Luis Obispo
County, a last outpost of good, open country, not yet
covered by the human plague, our leaders and representatives are eagerly promoting whatever will bring
the human plague.

As one of the "half per cent" referred to by Senator
Sturgeon, I am hoping that his unabashed assessment
of local conservation strength will wake people up to
the need for more conservation strength.

As always, Kathy applauded McMillan's sentiments as well as
his prose. Aware that she was already considered something of a
scold, Kathy refrained from writing letters of protest. Instead, she
urged allies like Steve Clensos to do the job for her:

The senator and Nipomo

To the editor:

Senator Sturgeon does not know his county very
well if he feels that 99 1/2 % of the public is in favor
of the proposed behemoth power plant in the
Nipomo "wasteland." The public here loves this
county for its beauty, its health-giving air, land and
sea. It is hardly a poor county, though no county is
without its share of needy. To reshape the county
for the ubiquitous needy — plus for some not-so-

> needy higher-ups — is a will o' the wisp . . . the
> lower taxes that will presumably result very soon
> turn out to be fool's gold.
>   Morro Bay has been sacrificed to the almighty
> buck, and so will Nipomo? . . .

Kathy grabbed her newspapers every day, observing that replies were quickly mustered in opposition to Clensos' letter. Mrs. Pauline Austin of Oceano, who appears to have arrived late to the fray, asked, "Why did the Sierra Club and its allied bodies not protest the purchase and eventual utilization of the site at the beginning instead of waiting all these years?"

Charles Anders wrote: "A few weeks ago Mrs. Jackson, whom I greatly respect and admire, asked the interesting question—in a broadcast, later reported in the press—'who shall decide?' . . . I recently approached 60 individuals on this matter—some known to me and many whom I never before contacted in any way—and every one of the 60, all of whom resided in Oceano, only a few miles from the proposed site, were strongly in favor of the plant being erected on the site."

Hastening to reply, Al Kulsar of Atascadero answered: "We have just completed a survey of 60 nature lovers, who we felt certain would agree with us, and surprisingly, they all did." He continued, "The dear lady, who felt that the Sierra Club has no business on the Dunes with their stupid progress-stopping protests, must be reminded that it was screwballs like these that saved the giant Redwoods from commercial gluttony. We would like to remind those who are inclined to rhapsodize about the dreamy smoke-stacks, and the jobs they represent, that California's scenic values are its most lucrative asset. . . . Tourists are not inclined to travel cross country to view smokestacks and electric towers. . ."

Kathy worked behind the scenes, relaying items from the Sierra Club in San Francisco to local newspapers, pounding out news releases about local activities on her little green Hermes. News from San Francisco was encouraging. The national board of directors of the Sierra Club met in April and recommended the preservation of the Oceano, Nipomo, Oso Flaco and Pismo Dunes. State officials of the California Association of 4-Wheel Drive Clubs were in interested attendance.

The releases she composed for local consumption were proper and formal; nonetheless they promised excitement to those who would join her hikes onto the dunes. In announcing one July hike, she quoted a past participant, a naturalist named Charles O. Blodgett, who declared that "a whole earth story starting with the ancient ice ages was waiting to be deciphered from the dunes; where, according to biology professor John Haller of the University of California at Santa Barbara, plants were flourishing "never found anywhere else in the world." As an added appeal to treasure hunters Kathy noted that a San Luis Obispo man found a white arrow-head fashioned from hard stone called a chert during the last hike. For those concerned that the outing would be too strenuous, she wrote that on the last hike ages ranged from three months to seventy-six.

Her monthly beach hikes, designed to cover every inch of San Luis Obispo County coastline, often attracted forty or more hikers. When she was scouting prospective routes she sometimes approached startled home owners, asking if it would be all right if some mild-mannered Sierra Club-types might please cross through their back yards on an upcoming Sunday? Thus she was able to work around some tricky areas in the community of Pismo Beach, where sharp bluffs topped by ocean-view homes forbade hiking at water's edge.

Kathy celebrated when the Santa Barbara Chapter of the Sierra Club, the parent to the Santa Lucia Group, voted to flatly oppose an atomic power plant on the dunes. Fred Eissler was probably instrumental in that decision. She hastened to relay the vote to the newspapers, as an effort to safeguard against any attempt by Lee Wilson to claim that the local Sierra Club favored such a plant.

But the crossfire, the rumors and the delays were wearying.

Even her most ardent supporters sometimes became discouraged.
On June 19, Bill Denneen of Nipomo wrote to her:

> The word I have is that PG&E is going
> ahead in about a month at the present
> site in the Dunes. That would be terri-
> ble as it is in the center of the best
> of the Dune area. We might have to com-
> promise to save the best part.
>
> Can we compromise at all? The Sierra
> Club is accused by the Santa Maria
> Times of "not giving an inch." If we
> could come up with a good compromise, I
> think we would get more local support
> and save the most valuable part of the
> Dunes. I suggest we try to save Oso
> Flaco Lakes and the Dunes north to
> Pismo Beach State Park. This would give
> us the best of the whole area...

To which she replied, on the twenty-first:

> In reply to your question: "Can we com-
> promise at all?" I believe the answer
> is a firm, persistent, dedicated
> "No"... School districts needs or eco-
> nomic stress are not even factors in
> making a decision to preserve unique
> valuable natural resources. Should the
> farmers have been permitted to continue
> sowing and reaping by compromise in,
> let's say, "just one corner of the
> floor of Yosemite Valley"? Should we
> compromise at Point Lobos, use half of
> it for a state park and half of it for
> establishment of a sardine cannery? In
> the Grand Canyon should we compromise

> and condone Marble Canyon Dam, but not
> Bridge Canyon Dam?...
>
> You state that the Sierra Club is
> accused by the Santa Maria Times of
> "not giving an inch". For my part, I
> congratulate us that we have earned
> this accusation — from those who do not
> hesitate to use up <u>now</u> what we should
> bequeath as a heritage to future gener-
> ations.

In the rest of her four-page letter, a copy of which she sent to Will Siri, she upheld the right of local newspapers to oppose Sierra Club plans, pointed out that their coverage had generally been fair and exhorted Bill Denneen to keep working.

Quite separately, dredging up her last reserves of energy, she fought off another corporate assault on the pristine purity of the dunes.

14

BAD CHEMISTRY

THE COLLIER CARBON AND CHEMICAL CORPORATION, a Union Oil subsidiary which had a refinery at the edge of the dunes along Highway 1, announced its intention to build a coking conveyor that would stretch across the dunes out to a commercial wharf that they intended to build. There, ocean-going freighters could pick up the commercial coke and haul it all over the world.

As Kathleen understood it, the coke was made by compressing heavy crude byproducts of the petroleum refining process. At that time it was being hauled on gondola cars by the Southern Pacific Railroad to Stockton where it was shipped to manufacturers of nylon stockings, fertilizer, and other petroleum-based products. To minimize the problem of dust, the company was required to spray the coke, then cover all gondola cars in transit. Collier hoped to eliminate this costly procedure by transporting the coke across the dunes to a pier for loading ships.

Kathleen anticipated that black coking dust would besmirch the dunes up to a distance of three or four miles. Additionally, the pier was a dubious prospect. Historically, turbulent surf in the area, compounded by frequent violent storms, had left very few such constructions standing. The result was usually a clutter of dangerous pilings and timbers, scattered for miles down the coastal beaches, threatening ocean traffic, wharves, piers and structures— creating a domino effect.

In an effort to experiment with the practicality of the project, Collier erected a mockup of a support tower out on the dunes.

Sierra Club members soon ran across it. Thus it became a regular stop on the Sunday dune walks, presenting Kathy with the perfect opportunity to expound on the perils inherent in such a conveyor.

Once again, members of the Santa Lucia Group were by no means unanimous in their reaction to the scheme. Dissension within the Group threatened to spill over into public view. On June 25, Kathleen wrote a letter to Will Siri.

> Re: NIPOMO Dunes (trouble within Santa Lucia Group Executive Committee)
>
> I am sorry to report that Lee Wilson's behavior is getting out of hand. It is conduct unbecoming a member of the Sierra Club. I am now convinced that things can only go from bad to worse.
>
> I am definitely worried and extremely uneasy since his telephone blast to me yesterday morning — when he phoned me long distance from the Orcutt Oil Field.
>
> I do not know what he can do to harm me personally, but he might possibly cause a public stir that would be very bad public relations for the Sierra Club.
>
> I have tried to overcome my feelings of inner alarm, but intuitively I feel uneasy and cannot put from me a sense of trepidation — but over what I am not sure. While in San Luis Obispo today I talked to one of our members who said: "You realize, don't you, Kathy, that there is a campaign to oust you, which is highly organized?" I said, no, I did not realize this at all. The member

went on to elaborate that a great deal of telephoning had been done by certain individuals in our Santa Lucia Group Executive Committee to plan action which would "get Kathy out of the way".

Our Group publicity chairman, Doreen Case, is on vacation and wrote, asking me to handle my own publicity in her absence. I did so. The enclosed brief, pleasant announcement came out in the S.L.O. TELEGRAM-TRIBUNE Wednesday, just a routine write-up. But Lee Wilson telephoned me Thursday morning and tore me apart with harsh, vituperative and untruthful statements simply because the news item had called the hike "a Santa Lucia Group hike." It is one of our Group hikes. It was passed by the Group Outings Committee, accepted by the Chapter Outings Committee, has been printed in our Group Bulletin along with other Dunes Group hikes ... The Dune hikes have been regularly publicized by our Santa Lucia Group publicity chairman in county newspapers.

Lee subscribes to the Paso Robles Press, so he will receive this issue (which she included with the letter) tomorrow... When he reads the paragraph in which I describe how our last Sunday's hike walked along the route of the proposed conveyor and considered the possible unsightly result of the operation in the Dunes, and that the unanswered question was raised about possible pollution of Pismo Clams and

sea-perch from possible spillage of
coke, I am afraid Lee will absolutely
explode.

My husband feels I should not talk with
him or allow him to talk with me any
more on the telephone. Duncan also sug-
gests that I tell you that he is beginning to turn over in his mind the pos-
sibility of consulting our family
attorney to see if there is cause for
complaint from Lee's harassment and
defamation of my character. You see, we
have four telephones in our home and
Duncan frequently listens to my Sierra
Club business conversations at my
request; his sensible and intelligent
advice has been of great help.

Lee's veiled threats; "People are up in
arms. They have stood all they are
going to of your vicious attacks on
Collier Carbon's conveyor and pier. I
told you from the beginning not to
fight the conveyor and pier. I gave a
lot of suggestions to you and Siri, but
you never followed any of them. People
are up in arms. They are going to take
action."

No, Will, the situation has gone beyond
being "patient and sympathetic" as your
last letter suggested with regard to
certain members of the Santa Lucia
Group executive Committee. I do not
know what they will try to do. My spirit truly is strong, but I feel an unac-
countable apprehensiveness. I know this

matter should be thoroughly investigated
without delay. I just know it.

It is hard enough to fight a conservation battle even with splendid help.
These unpredictable attacks of opposition take me by surprise, pull the rug
out from under me, are withering and
debilitating in their effect. I so des-
perately need my physical strength and
mental clarity for the job to be done.

(Kathleen then detailed the kind of intensive schedule she had
been following:)

Wednesday night I was on long distance
for almost an hour talking with George
Ford, Supt. of Collier Carbon: a gentleman fighting fair and square,
although very critical of our Sierra
Club attack. An extremely important
conversation, during which I took notes
fast.

Wednesday night I talked long distance
with Fred Eissler a very long time
about strategy.

Wednesday night I took one batch of
letters to the train to catch the 1:45
a.m., another batch to the 3:30 train,
and the last batch to the 6 a.m. outgo.

Thursday: some sleep; and more planning
and writing.

Friday, today: an hour and a half in
consultation with our County Planning
Director: and a short interview with

Secretary of the Port San Luis Harbor
Commission.

It is for these things I need my energy
— not for withstanding destructive
opposition — not for combating a
strange fear. Please call me.

Kathy

Kathleen was aware that employees of Collier Carbon attended her dune walks. She knew who they were; when she concluded
her argument against the proposed plan, she invited them to state
their case to the audience. As they did so, respect grew on both
sides. She was gratified when two of them eventually joined the
California Native Plant Society.

Eventually, she was enormously relieved when, after making
persistent complaints to the State Lands Division, she was advised
by its director on July 14, 1967 that Collier Carbon and Chemical
had dropped its plans for building a shiploading facility at Nipomo
Dunes.

It was not the environmentalists who forced the change, as
Kathy revealed years later in an oral history interview for the Sierra
Club: "It was the Southern Pacific Railroad. They saw themselves
losing a lot of business if the coking conveyor was built, and flatly
refused permission to construct a conveyor 'up and over' their
mainline out to the dunes."

But for much of the time, she was forced to remain vigilant and
fight on two fronts—threatening to blur her focus.

15
LOW PRIORITY

WHEN KATHY SCANNED THE PAPERS FOR NEWS about the dunes she occasionally would find something that amused her, such as an item reprinted from an AT&T employee newsletter: "Wanted: Man to work on nuclear fissionable isotope molecular reactive counters and three-phase cyclotronic uranium photo-synthesizers. No experience necessary." Remembering the young man at the Humboldt plant, she chuckled.

What she was looking for was an important announcement from the State Park Department. The previous November California voters had approved Proposition One, which authorized $85 million in bond money to be set aside for acquisition of State Park lands. Of course, Kathy hoped a good share of it would buy land in the dunes. Surely out of such a vast sum of money there would be enough to buy a substantial, reassuring tract in the dunes. She knew that bureaucratic wheels move very slowly, but by mid-year she was becoming eager.

When she located pertinent statistics or got a new idea her little Hermes typewriter gushed a stream of letters to the Sierra Club and the State Parks Department; she appeared at all county planning sessions and made it a point to attend every single supervisors' meeting—whether the dunes were on the agenda or not.

Meanwhile, the daily headlines in 1965 mirrored her inner turmoil. Edward R. Murrow and Adlai Stevenson dead; followers of Martin Luther King brutally attacked by state police in Alabama, mounting protests against the carnage in Vietnam. The streets full of rioters in the Watts area of Los Angeles.

But even as a citizen of the world who empathized with the troubles of the oppressed she was never tempted to view her own trials as trivial in the face of the world's sorrow or anarchy on the streets. Her wild wind-sculpted dunes had to be preserved, more important than ever as a permanent place of beauty, a refuge from the gyrations of a reeling planet.

Not the least of her private torments was the growing dissension spawned by the PG&E dispute within the Santa Lucia Group. Along the trail hikers had shared campfire stories, food, bad weather, splendid sights, occasional hardships, hearty laughter—always with a passion for preserving the wonders of nature. Little by little the cold winds of acrimony swept through the group as individuals' devotion to conservation faded in the face of dollar signs.

Kathy suspected that letters to members were being circulated by Lee Wilson's wife. They hinted that Kathy and Duncan were motivated by selfish concerns, that in some way they stood to gain if PG&E went elsewhere. Some of Kathy's old friends, like Claire Hardiman, reacted indignantly to these calumnies and disposed of them on the spot, but others like Kit Walling, who had led many hikes onto the dunes, dropped Kathy flat.

This was a new experience for Kathy. She was able to stand toe to toe with executives from PG&E or Collier Carbon and fight fair; she withstood letters of opposition from the community—to the point of defending every person's right to express his or her opinion. But in her entire life she had never been the target of the kind of hate that can exist between former friends. Sometimes at chapter meetings tempers ran so high that some members simply broke into tears.

More and more often the polite, patient, respected Lela Burdett stood between Kathy and Lee Wilson. Sometimes literally. Lela had agreed to become the next group chairman—a pledge that probably kept the group from breaking up completely.

Kathy would always insist that Lee Wilson counted on receiving large contracts for his electrical business if PG&E built a plant on the dunes. When she challenged him pointblank on the subject, he repeated his bland denials. Kathy didn't believe him. She knew he had been meeting privately with county supervisors and planning officials, exercising a persistent influence that she feared would win the day.

One notice she found in the San Luis Obispo newspaper seemed to increase the pressure. In early August the City Council of Guadalupe, the small agricultural town just south of the Santa Maria River in Santa Barbara County, announced that it was urging town citizens to write to PG&E with the suggestion that they would welcome an atomic generation plant on the beaches near their town. This caused massive alarm to the north. What if their rich neighbor snatched their tax plum right off the tree, before they could harvest it?

She approached the last supervisors' meeting in September of 1965 with apprehension. Would her months and years of work pay off? The State Park acquisition program authorized by Proposition One was bound to be on the agenda. As a means of ensuring local input, Sacramento had asked the county planning office to draw up a list of recommended state park sites in San Luis Obispo County. Ned Rogaway, the county planning director, had let it slip that this meeting would be pivotal. Rumors hinted at a supervisorial coup. What could it be?

As she entered, the clerk handed her a copy of the six-page letter that had been sent by the supervisors a week before to Fred Jones, the director of the Department of Parks and Recreation in Sacramento. It was San Luis Obispo County's prioritized list of potential state park sites.

A glance at the supervisors' list caused Kathy's stomach to churn. At the top of the list was a camping area at Pine Top Mountain in the northernmost part of the county, hardly close to where the people lived. Next came several suggestions for massive improvements to the Hearst Castle and Montaña de Oro parks. Down near the bottom, Number 11 requested that some land—not much—be added to the Pismo Beach State Park. It specifically stated: "Additional acquisition of sand dunes, including those within the PG&E and Union Oil properties, are considered unnecessary since agreements between the affected companies would provide possible use of the property without acquisition."

Number 12 suggested acquisition of Oso Flaco Lake, although the document almost dismissed its importance by mentioning that the area was remote, Union Oil was accommodating about allowing access, and state-wide interest among potential park users might not be too high.

How could they say that when each weekend the immediate area attracted dune buggies by the hundreds?

In essence, the Board of Supervisors was telling the State Park Department that it wanted nothing to do with the dunes. And with it went the sub-text—if San Luis Obispo County doesn't care, why should you?

Clearly people did care, because about a hundred of them were there. Some were conservationists like Kathy, anxious to be heard. Others were representatives of various chambers of commerce, desperate to prevent State acquisition of the dunes. Still others represented school boards who were already drawing up plans in their minds for improving gymnasiums and hiring new teachers when PG&E built their palace of power.

Kathy was aware that all eyes were on her, waiting for some reaction. She was determined to keep the turmoil within her breast in check: the shortness of breath, the pressure of tears welling in her throat, the rage that wanted to color her cheeks; none of them would be allowed to surface. Her mother's lessons about lady-like behavior were never more valuable.

When he gaveled the meeting to order, Board Chairman Fred Kimball disappointed the audience by announcing that this would not be a public hearing and that only limited testimony would be taken.

Then the board went on record as preferring the improvement of existing facilities over acquisition of new ones. Seemingly uncomfortable with the list, Ned Rogaway tried to explain to the supervisors, "If our tack is going to be to develop existing parks, Proposition One moneys won't do it. We're going to be hard pressed in the future to get money for acquisitions."

Supervisor Sam Borradiri pointed out that the money had been voted for acquisition and nothing else. He protested that San Luis Obispo County would be paying its share, so it should get its share of park lands.

Kathy was left squirming in her chair; it had previously been agreed that Lela Burdett would be the spokesman for the Sierra Club. In the five minutes allotted to Lela she politely told the supervisors that more parks and beaches must be acquired for future generations. Quoting from the best statistical evidence available at the time she noted that there would be 350 million people in the country by the year 2000. The population would be three-fourths urban with families averaging $10,000 a year income. Workers, she said, would work an average of only 32 hours a week. As she read her testimony, Kathy kept thinking how *she* would rouse the crowd—if she had been allowed to speak.

Reporters kept a close eye on the one person in the room who stood to lose the most—Kathleen Jackson. A photographer snapped her picture. Clad in a suit, accessorized by round, flat pearl earrings and a scarf, she stares through her glasses at someone who is speaking, her lips pursed tightly, her jaw jutting forward. The effort to stanch tears is apparent. Beneath the picture is a caption: "Kathy Jackson contemplates the plan."

Some noted that in a far corner of the room Lee Wilson sported a small grin of satisfaction as he picked imaginary lint on the knee of his pantleg. He looked like the fox who, after a lively chase, had cornered his prey.

16

THE DELUGE

HOW QUIET THE HOUSE WAS! Nobody was splashing in the pool, nobody was making popcorn in the kitchen, nobody was dashing off to practice for a school event.

The children had whirled into Kathy's life without warning; they departed just as abruptly. Some went to school, others were swept onto the road, to become part of the 60's counterculture. And Duncan wasn't welcoming them back home. Except for Michael and Gay, he declared he wanted nothing more to do with them. Kathy missed them, and missed their presence as buffers between herself and Duncan.

As Kathy climbed the stairs from the garage the only sound in the house was Duncan at the piano. Through the years she had learned to gauge his mood from the piece he was playing at the time. This wasn't Chopin. No, he was fidgeting with some discordant Stravinsky theme which she didn't care for particularly. And he probably had been drinking. He generally was.

Entering the living room, for a moment she considered pouring herself a drink, too, but —thirsty after a long day of talking— she opted for a glass of water. "I have some good news," she announced.

Duncan lifted his fingers from the piano. "Yes?" But his continuous stare at the score in front of him made it clear that her interruption was unwelcome.

"Yes," she said brightly. "About forty people will be going to the

State Park hearing in Sacramento. Most of them are from the Santa Barbara chapter. We've got to counter the San Luis Obispo Supervisors. Lyle Carpenter and Fred Kimble are going up, to testify against the dunes. I'm getting rides lined up for everyone."

He stopped, placed his hands deliberately in his lap and said, "Well, don't line up anybody with me. I'm not going."

"Not going? I already promised some people you would drive them in the Cadillac."

"Not going, Kathy. Not going. I'm not going to go up there, stand around all day with a bunch of dune rats, waste my time."

"But Duncan, you know how much I count on you."

"Count on my money, you mean. Dunes, dunes, dunes . . . tunes, tunes, tunes." He shifted into an angular, seemingly angry Aaron Copland piece that he had just learned.

"I've been working hard all day, Duncan. It's not fun to come home to an unpleasant house."

"Unpleasant! It's been forever since anything pleasant happened in this god-awful barn. You're never here. You never ask about my problems. My trees are dying. The drought is killing the almonds. We're losing a lot of money."

"Yes, yes, I know," said Kathy.

"No, no you don't! The only thing you care about are your damn sand piles. You are obsessed. Nothing else matters—nothing!"

In her shaking hand, the glass of water rocked like waves breaking on the beach. In her usually level head something broke. Kathy gritted her teeth, advanced toward Duncan and flung the glass of water into his face.

Water splashed across his bald head, trickled down his brows. He was too stunned to move. Slowly and deliberately he pulled a handerchief from his pocket, removed his glasses and mopped his face and checked for moisture on the piano keys. Then for a long moment they maintained eye contact, but said nothing.

Finally, Duncan broke the silence. "You know Kathy, that this isn't working any more, don't you?"

"Yes," she said sadly. Deflated, she sank into a chair. "It isn't working." After more silence, during which she fiddled with her empty glass, she asked, "Do you want a divorce?"

"Yes," he said quietly. "I do."

Then silence enveloped the room, practically sucked the oxygen from it.

After a few minutes he asked, "Will you trust me with the details, Kathy?"

"Of course, you're an excellent businessman. And known to be a man of your word." Duncan was cold as ice, but unlike Ali was above reproach in his business dealings.

"I'll take care of everything. I'll see the attorney. We'll draw up an agreement that will be fair. If you don't want to work you will have an adequate amount of money to take care of your needs. But if you want to work, I will structure things so that would be to your advantage."

It was clear to her that he had been formulating a plan for some time. But it didn't matter. "Do you want me to pack, leave right away?"

"That won't be necessary. I realize your work is at a crucial stage. This is a big house—enough room for both of us. There's no rush—and no need to announce the break-up. I'll leave it to you to pick the right time to move out."

17

THE PRICE OF VICTORY

OUT OF THE BLUE CAME CHEERING WORD. The State Department of Parks in Sacramento, ignoring the negative appraisal of the dunes by the San Luis Obispo County Supervisors, late in 1965 issued its own "Baxter Report" ranking the Nipomo Dunes a sizzling Number Seven on its priority list of land to be acquired for future parks.

Although two of the opposition supervisors had appeared personally at the Baxter hearings to urge total elimination of the dunes, a counter-lobbying effort behind the scenes by powerful forces in the Sierra Club and Conservation Associates had borne fruit. Because of their high price tag—$7.5 million—the dunes were not included in the initial Parks allocation of $150 million. But their prominent ranking signaled a good omen for the future

The setback to the anti-dunes faction at Sacramento was not accepted calmly in Kathy's Santa Lucia group. Kathy wrote a letter to Bill Deneen, recounting the local sequel. Lee Wilson, reporting to the group about a meeting of the Sierra Club he had recently attended in Los Angeles, declared that Fred Jones, Parks Department chief, had been present and had slammed the door on the dunes. According to Wilson, Jones dismissed the dunes as a "dead issue" to be "filed away and forgotten."

Kathy described what followed:

```
Lee then used inaccurate words to
describe the famous Baxter Formula
```

Report. He said they just tossed a lot
of questions into an IBM machine and
the Dunes came out what he called "seventh class," and was "knocked down to
58th place" and "dropped"— Oh, boy, was
I furious. I sat there just waiting
until he had finished and then said to
Madame Chairman Lela Burdett that I
would like to clarify the Baxter Report
— so I did. And I said, "The Dunes were
not rated seventh class, but 7th from
the very top of all the state park projects in Calif. — and that they only
got a 58 rating on the angle of COST."
Lee glowered.

Our new members who were present were
eating it all up and asked again: "Is
that really the way state parks are
chosen?" And Lee said quickly: "Yes—
that's the way."

And Lela called for order.

How can Lee call himself a S.C. member
and talk the way he does?

When the State Parks Department held a regional hearing
January 14, 1966 in Santa Barbara, Kathy rounded up plenty of
people to testify in favor of the dunes' inclusion in the state's mas-
ter plan—prestigious people from the Sierra Club and
Conservation Associates, and from the Federation of Western
Outdoor Clubs; eloquent people like Eban McMillan.

She also inspired Martin Litton to run an article about the
beauty of her dunes in his February issue of *Sunset* Magazine.

Clearly the momentum had shifted to Kathy's side. But the

Sierra Club directors were not yet on record about the question of preserving the dunes. And although Club leaders had been meeting regularly with PG&E executives, including Board Chairman Robert Gerdes, she knew from Ken Diercks that the utility giant had still not settled definitely on an alternate site.

It appeared that a deal had been worked out with a man named Bob Marre, at a site northwest of the dunes well past the village of Avila. The Marre family had owned the land clear back to a Mexican land grant. It was operated as the Marre Land and Cattle Company. Marre would not agree to PG&E's first choice of a site; it was too close to his house.

Farther northwest was a small, oak-filled area called Diablo Canyon. This locale offered important advantages. A plant here would not intrude on residential areas or industrial development. There was no public road to the site; few people had seen it who hadn't flown over it. Until it was chosen, Kathy had never been there.

The deal was very complicated since Marre refused to sell the land outright. Rather, he preferred an elaborate lease, which would give him the right to borrow up to six and a half million dollars at the same low interest rate paid by PG&E.

The alternate arrangement still had to pass muster with the leadership of PG&E and the Sierra Club, so the utility chartered a Lear jet to bring its executives and Sierra Club directors on an inspection tour. Kathy waited on the tarmac at the San Luis Obispo airport. She knew the Sierra Club directors and greeted them with effusive enthusiasm. When Ken Diercks introduced her to PG&E executives her sincerity and warmth were just as genuine.

"Oh, and there's something else. Would you believe that this airplane belongs to Frank Sinatra?" asked Diercks, glowing with Irish enthusiasm. "And this gentleman," he said as he pointed to the last person to exit the plane, "is Danny Kaye! He was the co-pilot!" Kathy replied with a polite, but blank expression. Not much for celebrity or films, she had no idea who Kaye was.

However, nobody else noticed her bewilderment. "Ken, how'd you set this one up?" asked Bill Johns, one of the PG&E executives. "That really ought to impress the Sierra Club folks."

"I had no idea," replied Diercks. Just a coincidence. But he was beaming.

Until this visit, surveyors and engineers visiting the site had done so in a rickety helicopter; its pilot always asked his passengers to own up to their weight—if one was too heavy, he couldn't take two. Diercks, knowing that Bob Gerdes would never hazard himself to such a contraption, brought in a better machine for the day.

However, some of the party had already bumped over bad roads in four-wheel-drive vehicles. The road was just a farm lane; it was necessary to open and shut fourteen gates to reach the Diablo destination. Kathy helped show the VIPs around, subtly hinting at the area's lack of scenic distinction. Lela and Bernie Burdett were there, but did not share her opinion. Having once hiked to a lovely little waterfall that graced the upper part of the canyon, they felt it was worth saving. However, weary from controversy, they said nothing.

Finally, on May 7, 1966, the Board of Directors of the national Sierra Club held their annual meeting at the Fairmont Hotel in San Francisco and rendered their judgment: "The Sierra Club reaffirms its policy that the Nipomo Dunes should be preserved, unimpaired, for scenic and recreational use, under State management, and considers Diablo Canyon, San Luis Obispo County, a satisfactory alternate site to the Nipomo Dunes for construction of an electric generating facility." The statement went on to add that marine resources should not be adversely affected, and that air pollution and radiation should not exceed certain limits. Lee Wilson did get one thing he wanted. It was specifically forbidden that high voltage transmission lines should pass through his beloved Lopez Canyon.

Of the fifteen Sierra Club directors, two abstained. Fred Eissler cast the lone resounding NO. Martin Litton was on a photo expedition to the Galapagos Islands; his absence would become particularly important.

By now, San Luis Obispo County residents were accepting the new plan. Few people had ever seen Diablo Canyon. Out of sight, never mind. The schools would get their taxes.

What was needed now was to persuade the Supervisors—as well as the California Public Utilities Commission and the federal Atomic Energy Commission—that Diablo was a good choice. Diercks called for Kathy's help as an expert witness.

By this time Martin Litton had returned from the Galapagos. He was not at all happy about what had transpired in his absence, sharing Fred Eissler's opposition to all atomic technology. Together they formed the Scenic Shoreline Preservation Conference to protest the choice of Diablo Canyon. Their plan was to appear at hearings of the California Public Utilities Commission and the federal Atomic Energy Commission—both of which were to be held in San Luis Obispo.

When Ken Diercks heard of the impending opposition, his people put together a slide show to be entered as evidence. It was meant to demonstrate that Diablo Canyon, although scenic, was not particularly different from similar oak-filled canyons along the coast.

At Diercks' request, Kathy directed them to a different canyon, but very similar to Diablo. Aerial photos were taken.

At the first hearing, Eissler and Litton testified that Diablo was a place of unique scenic beauty on the San Luis Obispo County shoreline. When shown slides taken by Diercks' crew, Eissler testified that yes, this was Diablo Canyon. Then it was revealed that the pictures were taken at a different place, so the claim that Diablo Canyon was unique did not hold water.

Finally, it was Kathy's turn to testify:

"People ask me why I believe the Nipomo Dunes are not a suitable place for PG&E's atomic power plant. I would like to state my belief. We need places where a man can be alone. Natural places, where man is a visitor, but does not remain. Our roots are natural, which we need to re-establish contact with our source, God, in a natural environment. We conservationists are not against progress, no, it is a matter of locating progress, plus the highest land use. I believe that with Diablo Canyon PG&E has found this location.

"I respect Mr. Eissler, although I disrespect his disloyalty to the Sierra Club. But I have to admire his integrity, resourcefulness, knowledge and dedicated drive. I will work with him, but perhaps not all the way.

"Because responsibility and conscience vary in human beings, we conservationists plan for all time and think about your successors and descendants. Therefore we must cooperate on vision: both for industry and for recreation. Open space is so rare. Let's hold onto it. It is akin to spiritual money in the bank.

"Look backward into your childhood, think about what was and is no more and can never be—not ever-ever-ever . . .

"It is a grave responsibility on the human conscience to alter forever a piece of God's earth. As engineers you know what has to be done: great beautiful miracles for the comfort and aid of man— but also, heartbreaking and terrible devastation."

When she finished, Ken Diercks ran up to her and asked for copies of her speech.

For many years, fellow conservationists would hold Kathy's complicity in the scheme to fool Fred Eissler and others against her. After Diablo Canyon, under the growing influence of David Brower the philosophy of the Sierra Club took a less conciliatory turn. The mantra became: Protest against industrialists and developers when we disagree with their choice of a site. But don't ever suggest an alternate.

Kathy felt uneasy about her part in the maneuver, but she promised Ken Diercks that she would help him if he would help her. By stretching the truth just a little, she had saved her beloved dunes.

Her frame of mind had almost settled into celebration, until — one day in September Kathy hurried, as usual, to answer the phone. It was a reporter from the *Telegram-Tribune.* "What do you know about this Sierra Club split?"

"Split? What do you mean?"

"Over Diablo Canyon. It just came over the wire. Says that they had a stormy three-hour session when Eissler and Litton tried to renege on the deal. Said the whole thing was cooked up in secrecy, against Sierra Club policy. Brower was in on it, too, but of course he couldn't vote."

"Did they vote?"

"Yes, but not until all kinds of charges had been flying around: of double dealing, bad faith, conspiracy. Finally the rebels were voted down nine to three. Seems most of the directors argued that a deal is a deal. Any comment?"

There was a long pause at Kathy's end of the phone. She felt as though she had been bashed in the back of the head with a shovel. "Just say that I'm concerned that the dissident directors could possibly try to start a citizens' group opposed to Diablo Canyon. If they do, I believe this would be disloyal to the Sierra Club."

Now her triumph had turned to ashes. Had she been the cause of an irreparable rift in the Sierra Club? An organization that she preferred over any organized religion?

18

AH WILDERNESS

KATHY'S SKILLED FINGERS WERE FLYING as she rushed to finish typing some legal briefs for Andy David's law office in Arroyo Grande. After more than four years of struggle for the dunes her tensions were easing, almost to the point of normalcy. The part-time job suited her well: the hours were good, her typing chores merely demanded accuracy, the other women in the office were agreeable. Because she worked in the afternoons she had plenty of time to devote to her Sierra Club correspondence. After three months her office manager, Anne Waiters, assured her that very soon now Mr. David would probably formalize the casual arrangement into a permanent agreement.

Everybody else had left at five o'clock. She looked up to see the proper attorney headed toward her desk.

"Would you please come to my office?"

"Of course," she replied brightly, flashing her habitual smile. Out of habit, she grabbed a steno tablet and pen, ready to take notes if he wanted to dictate something.

"Have a seat."

"Thank you."

"Do you like working here?"

"Oh, I like it just fine. Anne is very capable."

"And the other girls? How do you get along with them?"

"I like them fine. I don't think I've become close to any of them, but I feel harmonious with them."

He was looking out the window, not smiling. She realized something was wrong. "Do you really feel all right about being here?"

"I'm not sure what you would like to hear from me, but I'm comfortable. I have tried to do a good job."

"Yes, of course. But you're in the newspapers quite a bit. I hear from a number of people that you're spearheading that conflict about the dunes."

"That's true. I'm a very strong environmentalist. But I didn't think it was linked to my job. I came here to do my work, discharge my duties. My commitment to the environment is quite separate." The tears began to well in her eyes. "More of a personal responsibility to myself, to my own spirit."

Still with his back to her he said, "Well, that sort of thing won't work here. Take your things as you leave. Anne will send your check to your house."

Just like that. Kathy had not been prepared for the way many people now regarded her. Was she being treated differently because she no longer had Duncan's prestige to protect her? Now that she was no longer a rich woman? Perhaps.

This was not her first rebuff on the employment front. When she made her decisive move from Paso Robles to Arroyo Grande a few months earlier, an executive from Bechtel, the construction firm bidding to build the Diablo plant, had offered her a secretarial job. Tempted by the good salary, she was advised by friends that perhaps Bechtel wanted her on the payroll to silence her. No, she couldn't work for an organization that might oppose her efforts. At the same time, her friends told her—as gently as they could—that it was time to switch her registration from the Republican to the Democratic party, generally more sympathetic to matters of environment. Yes, her life was changing.

Her first job after the divorce had been for a Swiss restaurateur named Hartung, brought to the area to set up the new San Luis Bay Inn, then under construction. She helped him to organize a public relations program, assemble a mailing list of the most important people in the county and handle such matters as local favorites for a menu. But when it came time to open the Inn her boss told her, with regrets, that her services would no longer be required. Something about how the owners wanted to position themselves in the community. Didn't feel controversial people would help their public image.

So it had happened again. From Andy David's office it was not far to the home she had recently bought on Halcyon Road, perched on the edge of a hill. Her view stretched across fields of broccoli to the Oceano Dunes; on a fogless day she could see the ocean shimmering in the distance. But that evening the vista gave no comfort to an angry, tear-sodden Kathy. The usual pile of correspondence stacked next to her green Hermes did not tempt her. Little of consequence demanded her attention these days. She must await, with as much patience as possible, PG&E's decision about the land in the dunes. She felt certain they would sell it to the State Park Department, but when?

She couldn't turn to colleagues in San Francisco for comfort. All too many of them were blaming her for consorting with PG&E, the enemy. They said she shouldn't have testified, accused her of helping locate the Diablo site. Why, she asked herself, are they treating me like a traitor? There never was a more dedicated environmentalist on earth. Her beloved Sierra Club seemed to be splitting right down the middle and some thought it was her fault. She had sided with the "appeasers," the faction that felt it was possible—yea even their duty—to work with industry. Their opponents, led by the charismatic young Dave Brower and Fred Eissler, were just as firmly convinced that cooperation would lead to ever more destructive development. When she began her crusade, nuclear power plants were looked upon as a clean way to generate electricity—a way to save rivers from being dammed, to keep air free of fossil fuel smoke. But more and more often word was spreading about negative aspects of atomic energy. Children downwind from atomic testing done in the fifties in Utah and Nevada were showing evidence of thyroid conditions. More people were asking what would happen if a plant had a melt-down? What would be the long-term effects on people who worked at such places or lived nearby? Most alarming of all, nobody had figured a way to dispose of fuel rods. Opposition to the Diablo plant was growing more and more raucous by the day.

In her own community she was viewed more as a leper than a savior. How could people be so cruel? She had only tried to help. Didn't the compromise work in their favor? They got PG&E's power plant, and their dunes would remained unspoiled. Surely they could see the future tourism that would bring.

It began to dawn on her that she had paid a very high price for the dunes. Her lofty crusade seemed to have cost her a marriage, her respected position in the Sierra Club, and now—even the prospect of a comfortable, self-supporting old age.

Unaccustomed to feeling depressed, she spent nearly five days feeling sorry—really, really sorry— for herself.

It was nearly noon on the sixth morning when she sprang out of bed. "What is this? I'm only sixty-three. I've got a little money in the bank—and plenty of time because I'm not working. It's June, a glorious time for adventure. Why not take my money and spend it in a beautiful way, on something I've always wanted to do?"

What she wanted to do was backpack into the rugged High Sierras, in the area that nearly twenty years later would become the Golden Trout Wilderness. She wanted to feel the hot Sierra sun on her back, to thrill to mountain thunder, then tip her face up to feel the Sierra's fleeting afternoon showers course raindrops down her cheeks, to hear the melodious swoosh of the treetops as the wind tossed the pines. She wanted to identify every plant she could set eyes on, to gather cress by a brook for a salad. She wanted nature's healing power around her, underfoot, overhead.

Company would be nice. But none of the friends she approached was able to put his or her life on hold for a couple of months. Undaunted, Kathy proceeded to plan an expedition into the little-traveled heights all by herself.

She planned to start her trek from an undeveloped campground called Quaking Aspen, east of Porterville. Because she might be gone as long as two months, she carefully calculated how much dried food she would need, what sort of tent and bedroll, what kind of emergency medications. Her backpack couldn't hold enough, so she concocted a yoke to go over her shoulders—like a Dutch girl carrying pails of water—with two bags suspended from the yoke. She called the bags her "matildas." She would not listen to friends who advised that it was crazy for a 110-pound woman to try to carry eighty-five pounds of provisions. Nor could they talk her out of venturing into the high country alone.

A friend named Ulla Sontag drove her to the starting point, a trailhead at about 8,000 feet up in the Sierras, then watched dubiously as Kathy struggled down the path in the direction of the Kern River.

Within half an hour, Kathy knew she was in trouble. The heavy load was more than she could manage. Her first destination, a place called Jug Spring, was over eight miles away. Could she move her gear in relays, in hope it stayed intact? It would take all day and into the night.

Fortunately, a family of five motorcyclists came sputtering along. The father told Kathy to hop aboard; he would divide the transport of her provisions among his wife, son and two daughters. As much as she disapproved of motorcycles and the way they tore up trails, Kathy needed no coaxing. She climbed up behind the father and away they went. Safely delivered to Jug Spring, she thanked them and waved as they putted off into the distance.

No sooner had she straightened her gear when thunder rolled, clouds lowered and raindrops began to pound. She pulled out her tarp, erected a stick at one end, secured the borders and pushed everything she owned underneath it. Then she crawled under and stretched out. And it was wonderful. There she rested with her head in her hands—looking out at the big raindrops, feeling very cozy and very dry. It was an excellent feeling. She felt so satisfied to be in the wilderness, away from everything—even the dunes.

The next morning she began policing the area. In planning her trip she had written to the head ranger at the Inyo National Forest, explaining she would be exploring the area alone, enclosing an itinerary. She asked that the rangers keep an eye on her. In return she pledged to fill plastic bags with litter wherever she went. Forest Service trail crews could then pack the refuse out. The head ranger agreed; wherever she went she found plastic bags waiting. The enormous amount of litter she gathered never ceased to amaze her. That day it was noon before she could pronounce the Jug Spring area tidy.

About that time she looked up to see the motorcycle family return. The father explained they were concerned about her. She accepted their offer to haul her gear to the next campground, but she preferred to walk.

Thus, with the help of motorcyclists, an occasional horseback rider and other hikers, over the next few days she managed to get her heavy load to Kern Lake. It was a lovely place; long ago a landslide crashed into the canyon, damming a U-shaped lake. Surrounded by willows, the water was home to many ducks and an abundant supply of fish.

By then she concluded she would not be able to depend on the kindness of strangers to haul her gear for the entire trip. On arrival at the lake Kathy was delighted to find Betty, the wife of a packer named Woody who had assisted many Sierra Club High Trips with their gear. After exchanging a few pleasantries Kathy said, "I'm afraid that I have more equipment than I can carry. Do you think Woody could send me a burro? I have packed with burros on Sierra Club family trips. I can handle one."

Betty replied, "Probably. Woody'll be coming back in a few days. He'll bring you a burro, but you wait here for him here."

If Kathy expected the Sierras to be populated by fellow conservationists in awe of the wonders of nature, she was soon disabused of the notion. Betty was in charge of a group of dudes, dentists on vacation. Kathy watched in amusement as the tenderfoot crowd, unaccustomed to spending hours in a saddle, stretched their legs in pain. Their idea of roughing it, she discovered, included packing in three hundred pounds of ice to assure perfection at cocktail time! Their party that first evening was so boisterous that Kathy feared someone would drown in the lake.

Also camped near the lake was a coach with some of his students from Taft High School in the San Joaquin Valley; he was teaching them to fish. One evening they invited her to join them in a feed of fresh, crisply fried trout with corn bread. She relished every bite.

She met one other environmentalist, a tall, thin man in a battered hat. Henry Brown, cheerfully defying a limp thanks to his a long staff, had built a wilderness cabin farther up the Kern. He called it Fish Camp, not after creatures of the stream but after his mother's family who were named Fish. He promptly invited Kathy to visit and just as promptly she accepted.

In a few days Woody showed up and introduced Kathy to Sambo, a sturdy little mountain burro. Woody showed her how to tie what he called a squaw hitch to secure the cross-cradled saddle, which was equipped with two panniers for gear. Woody gave instructions on when to give him grain—not only for the animal's nutritional needs but also as a device to lure him back in case he slipped away.

She led Sambo up the trail, with Henry Brown's cabin as her first destination. Kathy and Henry got along famously; she even became friends with his wife Irene, a woman so shy that she fled into the woods at the approach of strangers. Kathy was charmed with Henry's teenage daughter, Emily; together they explored the surrounding territory.

Fish Camp was twenty-six miles from the nearest road. Most food and building materials had to be packed in, generally on the backs of mules or horses. Younger, fitter hikers could make it in one day; most people took two. It was a rough affair, built from logs, rocks and items to be found in the surrounding forest. For a long time its sole building was a storage house where food could be protected from marauding wildlife. But it was not without a few amenities. Henry had built a spring-fed bathtub. At the sight of it Kathy whooped with delight, stripped naked and jumped in, gleeful as a small child dashing into the surf. Henry, a man of Victorian morals, was at first dismayed, then beguiled by her utter lack of self-consciousness.

After she left the Browns' cabin Kathy spent the next few weeks exploring. Much of the time this most gregarious of women was alone, oblivious to the cougars and bears roaming the nearby canyons. Backpackers, returning that summer from places with exotic names like Shotgun Pass, Rocky Basin Lakes and Siberian Outpost brought home tales of a strange little woman with a burro who divided her attention between picking up cigarette butts and identifying wildflowers.

Occasionally Sambo would wander off in pursuit of a more delicious salad. She generally found him because a bell around his neck tolled his presence. But sometimes Kathy had to beat the bushes to frighten him so the tattling bell *would* tinkle.

Thus she spent the warm Sierra summer days, accompanied only by the buzzing of bumblebees, the cry of hawks, the flush of waterfalls, the scent of pine after rain. At night she enjoyed the company of stars, owls and the tinkle of Sambo's bell.

But as she walked, her mind frequently pondered an encounter which had taken place earlier in her trip, back at Kern Lake.

It was a long, lazy evening—on or near summer solstice. She sat looking at the lake, amused by trout leaping in pursuit of bugs hovering near the waters' surface, hypnotized by ever-widening circular ripples that ensued.

The moment would have been perfect, had it not been for a rowdy group of motorcyclists camped nearby. Obviously they had made room in their panniers for plenty of beer.

She looked up as a young man lurched toward her. Always open to strangers, she nevertheless experienced one moment of apprehension—the fellow looked rough.

He wasn't very tall; judging from his muscular build and the shape of his hands, his work was physical. He wore a plaid shirt and had a bandanna tied around his long hair. "Excuse me ma'am. May I join you?"

"Why yes, certainly." She was relieved that he seemed polite. "Are you enjoying it here?"

"Oh, this is the most wonderful place in the world."

He offered her a sip of his beer. Kathy smilingly declined. For a few moments they sat in silence. The camper, probably in his early thirties, looked puzzled. "This is wild, rough country. Not for, uh, mature ladies. You seem to be by yourself. How come?"

Somehow, Kathy sensed in his quiet manner a kindred spirit. Almost without realizing it she found herself telling him about the dunes, about how much she had always wanted to do this trip, how nobody could come with her. She asked, "Do you have a family?"

He nodded as he drained his beer, then savagely crushed the can between strong, callused fingers. Then he started to talk. Words fell in torrents.

"I live in Los Angeles, work for the city in the maintenance yard. I hate my job.

"My wife, she doesn't care for the out-of-doors. She just wants to watch soap operas and game shows all day. When I come home in the evening she cooks some kind of a meal out of a box or heats up a TV dinner. She's fat, talks nonstop on the phone to her friends about nothing. Hardly even says hello when I come home from work."

"Children?"

"My kids? I've got two of them. My wife won't let me keep them in line, so they sulk or yell at me. The only time they talk to me is when they want something."

She didn't try to stop him, or to comment as the sun finally disappeared behind a peak and darkness fell.

"Sometimes I feel like I'm stuck. Just stuck. I hate the city. Getting out like this—this is all I've got. If I wasn't able to get out sometimes, smell the pine trees, try to catch a fish, I think I'd just kill myself. Thank God for the wild places. And the people who try to keep them this way."

He stopped and stared at Kathy. "I don't know why I'm unloading all this on you. I've never seen you before. I'll probably never see you again. But you looked like you might understand."

He stood, brushed dirt and pine needles from his jeans, and disappeared into the darkness.

Kathy looked after him, buoyed by an unexpected epiphany. This fellow-child of the outdoors was the anonymous beneficiary of her long campaigns, the nameless but ubiquitous seeker after beauty who had always been on her mind when she fought to preserve nature. It was this fellow, who felt so "stuck." It was for him and the millions he symbolized that she had defended the dunes. So that for ages to come they could enjoy unspoiled retreats by the sea and in the mountains and canyons, pristine wildernesses where they could get away to think, dream, heal the torments of their crowded lives through the bounty of nature.

Suddenly she felt a vast relief. It had been a long struggle, banging her head against all those cold, stubborn walls. But it had not been for nothing.

19
LOVE IN BLOOM

THE WOMAN WHO EMERGED FROM FIFTY-FOUR days in the wilderness had a new confidence. She began signing her correspondence and referring to herself by her given name: Kathleen. Her friends, attuned to the difference, duly changed from "Kathy" to Kathleen. She became aware that her family name—Goddard— had achieved fame through a distant cousin, the aerospace pioneer Robert Goddard. She began to use it more frequently. Free to explore relationships again, she sought the company of various men—and occasionally women. This time she measured them by their opinions about nature, and the degree of their dedication to the earth's resources.

With her knowledge of bureaucratic systems, she was hired to open an office, to form a Medical Association for San Luis Obispo County's physicians. The work was part time, its nature uncontroversial.

And she had a good time. One friend, a state ranger at the Hearst Castle, planned a special party. Kathleen invited the "knap-suckers", her Sierra Club backpacking friends of so many years' duration, to a skinny dipping party by moonlight in the estate's enormous white and blue swimming pool known as the Neptune Pool—witnessed only by William Randolph Hearst's real and ersatz Roman statues.

The decision to build PG&E's atomic power plant at Diablo Canyon still rankled some Sierra Club members, but the ruckus was now focused on the controversial David Brower. As the realization of the plant grew more imminent, so did the public's protest against it. Nearly forgotten was the corporation's initial intention to build the plant on the dunes.

With her prodigious energy looking for a new cause, she helped to found a local chapter of the California Native Plant Society, dedicated to the identification, study and protection of native species. She attended Dr. Robert L. Hoover's botany courses in San Luis Obispo at California State Polytechnic College and learned to address plants formally, by their Latin names.

She looked forward to the first annual banquet of the organization, and was only mildly surprised to find herself the center of attention.

"Do you mean you went to the Sierras by yourself? How long were you gone?" asked one astonished friend.

"Seven and a half weeks."

"Weren't you afraid? Of mountain lions and bears?"

"I never saw any. Deer, of course, but nothing else."

Behind her back she heard a shrill female voice: "That's crazy. A woman in her sixties going out alone like that. I think twice before I even drive to San Francisco!"

Kathleen knew most of the people, but found herself seated at a table with a fellow she didn't know—who immediately caught her interest. Above his neatly trimmed white beard his eyes sparkled with wit. She noted that for a small man he could put away an enormous amount of food.

"My name is Gaylord Jones. I know you but you probably don't know me."

"You look familiar, but I'm having trouble . . ." she replied.

"My late wife and I went on some of your Sunday trips onto the dunes."

"Oh, I'm so sorry."

"It's all right. She died two years ago. I'm alone now."

The pained shrug of Gaylord Jones' shoulder bespoke a man

not totally cured of grief even as it invited Kathleen to change the subject. She did. "And what do you do?"

"I was an architect before I retired but now I'm a rock hound and photographer."

"And what do you photograph?"

"My goal is to photograph every wildflower that grows within sixty miles of my home in Santa Maria.

"What a fascinating project!" she responded with genuine enthusiasm.

They talked, they laughed, they even flirted. Before the evening was over it was agreed they would go hiking together on the dunes, the next day. The hikes became more and more frequent. She loved taking him to places she enjoyed, places the general public rarely visited. On one particularly genial afternoon, when they were discussing Gaylord's love of etchings, Kathleen flashed him a wink: "Would you like to come up to my place and see *my* etchings?"

Responding warmly to the old joke Gaylord replied, "With much pleasure, my dear."

In front of the fireplace at her house Gaylord put his arms around her and kissed her. Then he held her at arms' length by both shoulders, "You know, Kathleen dear, I'm ten years older than you are and I've been alone for some time. I'm not sure if this will work."

As she would tell friends years later, "It worked! He was loving, warm and we were ready for each other. He stayed the night. And then he stayed a lot more nights, too."

They were married in 1971 in a niche at the Presbyterian Church on Traffic Way in Arroyo Grande. Afterwards they had a simple reception at the Madonna Inn in San Luis Obispo. Then they excused themselves and left for a two-week honeymoon hike in the High Sierras, accompanied only by a pack burro named Hannibal. Their destination was Moraine Lake, where they took off their clothes and waded out in the moonlight among the knotweed. It was there that a nervous Gaylord owned up to a secret he had managed to keep from everyone for many years—he didn't know how to swim!

Kathleen had finally found a husband who shared her passions, who happily trailed along as she led hikes onto the dunes, who joined her causes, who was comfortable with the outdoors people she preferred. As long as he had a camera strap slung across his shoulder, he was eager to go anywhere. Together they explored the dunes, gave names to places like Hidden Willow Valley and to plants like Comet's Plume. Theirs was a loving (if sporadically bickering) union. And it would last twenty years until Gaylord's death when he was ninety-one. They became known as the People of the Dunes.

There was much to be done—and they did it together. Of critical concern was the ruinous impact of the motor vehicle people upon the rare flora in the dunes. As was her custom, Kathleen tried hard to see the riders' point of view. She knew from Greek mythology that somewhere deep in the human psyche the image of a powerful horse dashing through the surf was as deeply inbedded and as universal as the great sea god Triton himself. And if that urge had been transferred from a horse to a souped-up, homebuilt buggy it was nevertheless as powerful.

Most of these fellows worked hard at their jobs, built their machines in the garage at night, loved the smoky blue-gray fumes that spewed forth when a motor sprang into action, relished the feel of a fist clutching a wrench. They took great pride in their home-made buggies, usually combining a VW chassis and some form of air-cooled engine. They were delighted when a child or grandchild shrieked with glee as a buggy bounced across the sand. Were their emotions any less genuine than Kathleen's joy when she sighted a blossom unfolding?

Many of these people were kind, good-hearted, responsible citizens. Countless times they had helped her ferry an important visitor to his destination, one who had less fitness or time than a proper visit to the dunes required. She had to admit their willingness to travel great distances and give up their time to testify to various boards or commissions about why the dunes should become a state park.

But there was another element of motor people, ones who flew along on buggies dubbed "water pumpers," who were far less responsible. At a time when legal ownership of the dunes was unclear, they felt free to roam anywhere. Certain areas had been fenced off where No Trespassing signs were posted; they were run down and flattened. Fences that survived the shifting of dunes fell prey to wirecutters. Even worse, because angles of light slanting onto the sand can play optical tricks, over-eager, over-lubricated vehicle people were incurring grievous injuries. More than once a driver—convinced a flat dune lay ahead—plunged over the precipice, hurling man and machine down its slipface and into the pit of a barchan depression. Arms, legs and even necks were broken. Much blood was shed. To this day the dunes are littered with broken glass and twisted metal—witness to terrible accidents caused by too much speed and too little caution. And the landscape bears permanent scars where drivers, loving "run-downs," or areas where they could speed down the side of a dune, tore up all fragile life in their wakes.

Runaway buggy wheels can permanently shatter plant growth. Plants like the Beach Bur and Silver Dune Lupine survive by putting out extensive root systems. When wind shifts the position of a dune, uncovered roots run in parallel lines, like carefully laid underground cables. These life-extending "wires" send runners from which new growth is fostered. When dune buggies break these delicate connections, the plants are unable to produce a new generation. Then the dune is also in danger because these underground runners are instrumental in holding the sand in place.

Already the situation near Oso Flaco Lake was growing desperate. The dunes were becoming so bare of vegetation that they were moving into the lake itself, threatening to silt it shut. Although Kathy truly believed that education was the answer to almost all environmental problems, she recognized the impossibility of confronting the hundreds of campers and picnickers who arrived every weekend.

Instead, Kathleen and Gaylord drafted a coterie of friends to work with them on areas which were particularly endangered. One was the relatively unspoiled knoll the Joneses named Coreopsis Hill. Giant Coreopsis plants, resembling menorahs with yellow blossom "candles" extending from each branch, bloom there—and almost nowhere else on earth.

Gaylord had some signs made that showed a vehicle in the center of a circle, with a slash over it—an international symbol of "forbidden". Trudging across the dunes, he and Kathleen dragged hand-lettered signs warning vehicles to stay off. But they had scarcely planted them in the sand when vehicles rolled right over them.

Almost by accident, Kathleen and Gaylord discovered that they had a secret weapon—a weapon that made them far more effective than younger, more confrontational, volunteers.

One Sunday afternoon they unloaded their backpacks and waited for the convoys of sputtering vehicles they knew were headed their way.

"You, young man, you!!!" Kathleen screamed, trying to be heard above the roar of the unmuffled noise of a line of dune buggies headed right toward her. She did not budge from the center of the path where she stood.

"Move over, lady," shouted the lead driver—a fellow whose formerly muscular build now cascaded into a pot belly encased in a "Grateful Dead" tee shirt depicting snakes crawling out of a skull.

"Young man, you must not go up there!"

"Why the hell not?" He climbed out of his buggy, hauled himself to his feet, towering over her in a show of bravado for his fellow drivers. It wasn't his attitude, but his beery breath that set her back a couple of paces.

"There are rare and endangered plants there. Your tires will do great damage to their roots. This is a place of beauty. We belong to the California Native Plant Society and we're protecting those plants."

Conditioned, like most people, to show respect to older people, the fellow was finding it hard to get a word in edgewise. Finally he interrupted—"Nobody's going to tell me where I can or can't go."

Now Gaylord gimped forward, clutching his walking stick and limping—although normally he was as spry as a cricket. "Come now young fellow! Surely a man of your muscle can arrange to ride elsewhere." He waggled his stick imperiously.

The bruiser snarled some four-letter words—and immediately regretted them. Then his shoulders sagged. He looked to the next buggy and threw his hands up, "These old people are terrible. You can't fight 'em."

The buggy drivers turned their contraptions around and headed back toward the beach. Kathleen and Gaylord looked at each other and giggled. They had discovered that the worst blowhards in the world would seem cowards if they abused older people. Thus they turned their status as senior citizens into a formidable weapon.

20
WOMAN'S WORK IS NEVER DONE

THE BIG DAY FOR THE DUNES WAS AT HAND. The official announcement would be made in Los Angeles so Kathleen, as usual, helped to arrange the carpools to enable Sierra Club members from its Santa Lucia and Santa Barbara chapters to share in the glorious moment.

As Ken Diercks had long anticipated, the process of separating PG&E from its Nipomo beachfront holding had not been easy. But Diercks had felt an obligation to use his influence to see to it that the people he had been working with, and who had helped him, got what they wanted. By late 1974 he was feeling pretty good about the arrangement that had finally been struck. To his mind, everybody won: Conservation Associates, the Sierra Club and Kathleen got their dunes; PG&E got its atomic power plant; San Luis Obispo County got its taxes; the state got a new park. Not that PG&E had any intention of just handing over 1100 acres from the goodness of its corporate heart. By 1974 its CEO was Jack Bonner. The deal that Diercks made with Bill Mott, Director of State Parks, was that $1 million would be a fair price for the dunes and the Bodega Bay property (which was leased to the county of Sonoma for $1). Bonner did not agree. PG&E executive Bill Johns came to Diercks' aid by convincing Bonner that a good tax write-off would be included in the transaction. Bonner agreed, getting something extra for PG&E. The specifics of these elaborate negotiations interested Kathleen, even though she was rarely privy to such details.

When everybody arrived at the meeting place in Los Angeles, the mood was ebullient. Kathleen waved to friends, smiled, then sat next to Gaylord who clasped her hand. They were somewhat disconcerted to notice, in the audience, a goodly proportion of vehicle enthusiasts. Perhaps she should have anticipated that. After all, she had worked with them through the years.

When Mott stood up, the anticipation was palpable. "Today, I want to announce an historic first. Many of you in the audience have worked hard for this day to come true."

Kathleen couldn't help it. She clapped tentatively—then her companions joined in. She acted like an excited young cheerleader.

"This land, formerly owned by PG&E will not see an atomic power plant built on its beautiful shores."

More applause, even louder. Some foot stomping.

"Instead, I am here to announce that the land will become—forever—a part of the California State Parks System."

Kathy stood up. Tears were streaming down her grinning cheeks.

Her fellow conservationists stood with her, locking arms, patting backs.

Mott could barely be heard over the enthusiasm. "And I am here to announce that this will become the very first motor vehicle park in the state system!"

Kathleen continued to dance a little jig and applaud until her wrists stopped in mid-motion as she noted that those around her had abruptly sat down.

What had she just heard? A motor vehicle park? Further desecration of the dunes? There had been no hint from the Parks Department of this unwelcome cloud over her victory.

Across the aisle, the jubilation continued unabated as supporters of motor vehicle freedom danced with glee.

Her fellow Sierra Club members picked up their papers and jackets and filed out of the auditorium. A sober, subdued group of environmentalists drove back to San Luis Obispo. Almost nobody spoke.

At home with Gaylord, Kathy weighed her choices. The unexpected concession to the buggy riders was a blow, no question about it. But that was the nature of the beast, this kind of work was never done. Their concern was underlined by an event over the previous Labor Day weekend. Something called the Sandnationals had made a riotous impression at Pismo Beach. Because the deal with PG&E was still in limbo at the time, confusion had reigned. Enormous vehicles scattered tons of sand as they participated in drag races, a hill climb and obstacle course. Campers were supposed to be limited to 1200 sites but, with a wink, rangers were advising people to "camp behind the dunes, out of sight." They were particularly directed to the delicate shores of Oso Flaco Lake.

Kathleen feared the spectacle was an augury of worse times to come. What was to keep people from charging with their buggies anywhere they liked now that the area was designated as a vehicle park? The situation was compounded by the sprawling, disorganized nature of the dune buggy crowd. Dealing with PG&E there had been a visible structure, a Bob Gerdes at the top, somebody like Ken Diercks to call on the phone, somebody to ask for a meeting.

Yes, it was a blow. But she was not without resources. She had a willing partner in Gaylord, plus the experience accumulated in hearings and discussions. From her observation of the calm, adroit Ken Diercks she had picked up a useful tactical clue or two. One of Ken's most effective moves was to "befriend the enemy."

How could she get a handle on the opposition? The most reckless and belligerent of the Off Highway Vehicle (OHV) drivers disdained aligning themselves with any organization, preferring to blast over the landscape with no regard for authority. But she had made it a point to maintain her contacts with the relatively disciplined California Association of Four Wheel Drive Clubs, even though she knew many of their members still proudly sported those bumper stickers saying TO HELL WITH THE SIERRA CLUB. She might be able to work out a reasonable modus operandi with the Association's leaders if the people at the Park Department gave her a hand.

A fellow volunteer named Margaret Price invited Kathleen to her home to meet Garlan Salzgeber—everybody called him Gar— the new supervisory ranger for what was called the Pismo State Beach. She accepted, of course. Salzgeber was of medium height, had a reassuringly firm handshake, wore his uniform neatly. Although not physically overbearing, the man had an air of authority; she could imagine that a rough vehicle rider would listen to him. But why was he the person assigned to the dunes? Was it because he liked machines, wanted to be an advocate for the Off Highway crowd?

For his part, Salzgeber was a bit leery of Kathleen. After all, he had heard that she was the dynamic woman who had forced the mighty PG&E to relocate an atomic power plant. What would she do to him?

"I understand," Kathleen ventured. "that you're stretching a fence around the motor vehicle area."

"That's right," replied Gar.

"Why?"

"One of their people strayed onto private property, had an accident which left him a parapelegic, and sued—both its owner and us. We can't let them wander anywhere they want to any more."

Kathleen had heard about that. "What a shame it took such a terrible accident to corral them, but what about rare and endangered animals and plants?"

"I should hope," replied Gar, "that we can help by keeping the vehicles in their proper spot."

Kathleen pried out of him that his father had been a ranger before him, that he grew up on the beach at the Carpinteria State Park, that he loved to surf, back-pack, anything out of doors. She was impressed that he had recently completed a year as an exchange ranger in Yosemite National Park—an honor which should prepare him to understand both people and preservation.

But she determined to maintain a certain distance until she knew more. Found in her papers was a hasty note scrawled on a tablet, intended for use at a hearing:

> *Flying over South SLO County this morning I looked down upon the open wounds of the Nipomo Dunes. These have been caused by one user group alone: the recreation vehicle group. Nothing in the history of recreation, probably, has paralleled the violent, arrogant disregard of natural beauty and unique natural values the ravages of this contemporary species, the recreation vehicle user, has caused. Very simply, this noisy, polluting ORV recreation is a public nuisance.*

This was the position she would always hold. Even so, little by little Gar gained her trust. A comical story proved hard to resist. "When I stopped one good ol' boy redneck and told him he shouldn't be drinking so much he said, 'Hey, I wouldn't want to drive those dunes sober! They're too dangerous.'"

"But that's terrible! They do so much damage."

"Kathleen," said Gar with that note of authority she had come to respect. "It's about time you cut me some slack. Little by little, things are changing. When I came here ninety-five percent of the guys on the dunes were bad actors. People who wanted to play outlaw and thought a night in jail was just the price of a good time. My goal is to turn that around; someday ninety-five percent of the people will behave responsibly."

"Well," she responded, "That would be good."

"Kathleen, don't you see? We're on the same page."

She gave him her hug of friendship. Gar Salzgeber was doing his best. And although she would prefer to see dune buggies banished forever, at least they would be restricted under his stewardship. She had to face a hard fact of life. Because Off Highway Vehicle owners were required to buy annual licenses, called Green Stickers, they had built up an enormous fund in the state treasury. Supposedly this money was for the purpose of acquiring new land for additional vehicle parks. However, few people wanted such reputedly rowdy motorists near their homes, so land became difficult to acquire. In lieu of new land, money was diverted to improving facilities already owned—such as Pismo.

In the years to come, sometimes in the company of Gar, Kathleen and Gaylord explored every inch of the dunes, constantly delighted with the discovery of new places and plants. Dressed just alike in plaid yellow shirts of "coreopsis gold" with broad-brimmed hats and sturdy walking sticks they were a sight as familiar to snowy plovers as to the hundreds of hikers who followed them in search of new sights. Gaylord took thousands of pictures of the flowers.

They loved to pack their sleeping bags out onto the dunes on a moonlit night. In the '70s, when altering of perception was the rage, they didn't need chemicals to enter another reality. Under a full moon, shadows become difficult to interpret, footing tricky; giggling with glee, people stumbled around as though drunk which—in a way they were. Drunk with nature's special effects.

There would be good times, such as in 1976 when the California Coastal Act mandated that all public agencies should protect rare and sensitive habitats of plants and animals wherever they were known to occur. In that same year the California Department of Fish and Game declared that the Santa Maria River lowlands were one of the most important wetlands in the state in need of protection. It seemed that people were finally awakening to the need to preserve the area.

By 1980 a U.S. Fish and Wildlife report described the Nipomo Dune Complex as "the most unique and fragile ecosystem in the

State of California" and ranked it Number One on a list of forty-nine habitats in need of protection. That same year the U.S. Secretary of Interior designated the Nipomo Dunes as a National Natural Landmark. Each incremental step provided Kathleen with extra ammunition for her next skirmish.

By 1982, with the help of Gar, vehicles were no longer allowed onto the dunes through the entrance at Oso Flaco Lake. Eventually, vehicles were forbidden even to approach the area because the action of their wheels was changing the contour of dunes, threatening to fill the lake. Still, anyone who hikes high enough today can look down to see that on the ocean side of the state park fence vehicles have rendered the land bare, packed so hard that on most days even a two-wheel drive vehicle can negotiate the area without getting stuck.

Occasionally County Supervisors spoke so harshly to Kathleen in a meeting that she left it, to shed humiliated tears when she crawled into her car. But she always came back the next week. If the squeaky wheel gets the grease, Kathleen screeched like a rusty locomotive squealing her demands for attention. Some officials gave in without even a fight, preferring to concede rather than to subject themselves to her numerous phone calls. She had the disconcerting habit of calling officials at home, at meal time.

Ever eager to inform, to spread the good word, Kathleen never neglected an invitation to speak to school children, service clubs, church and civic groups. The message never varied: These dunes are yours. Enjoy them, protect them, fight for them.

Often, when she went grocery shopping a child would say, "Mother, that's the dune lady. She came to our school and talked about birds and flowers. It was cool." Kathleen would then make it a point to meet the parents, invite them to the dunes.

Sometimes she led young students to a special set of half moon-shaped barchan dunes. She ordered children to cross their arms and grab their opposite shoulders firmly with their hands. Then they must close their eyes, to keep the sand out, and roll like a log down the slip face of the dune. Down and around they tumbled, gleefully eager to scramble back up and do it again. No child could ever forget that close encounter with a real dune.

Gradually, others have taken up Kathleen's cause. The part of her that has long been obsessed, to the verge of fanaticism, lives on through the Thoreau-like character of her faithful disciple Bill Denneen. PG&E's Diablo Canyon plant became ever more controversial—especially after the near-disaster at Three-Mile Island in 1979. Protesting at the gates to the facility, then under construction, Denneen even got himself arrested and detained. But he was so totally convinced that atomic radiation damages the DNA-molecule and is too dangerous to justify any amount of electricity produced by that method that he didn't begrudge the jail time he eventually served.

Shirtless, ruddy, his long white beard tickling his chest, Denneen still leads strenuous hikes as far south as Point Sal; although in his seventies, he starts each leg of his hike by jogging friskily to the delight of his three dogs. Confrontational, he no longer belongs to organizations which he feels aren't single-mindedly dedicated to getting all vehicles off of the dunes—his ongoing crusade. He lives in a self-sufficient style on an acreage in Nipomo where he raises a garden and livestock. More as a gesture to the next generation than out of financial necessity he operates his home as a youth hostel. At any given time travelers from all over the world are treated to his hospitality—administered with a healthy dose of environmentalism.

The more moderate, patient, persistent side of Kathleen has been taken up by people like Jack and Grace Beigle. They also lead hikes and helped to found an educational nature center at the campground in Oceano—where most of the camping spaces are occupied by vehicle enthusiasts. Jack has become something of an expert on history—both natural and human. Grace's expertise is botany; she has even planted an extensive garden of dune plants near the nature center. They have been instrumental in putting together a wildflower guide to the dunes.

In the early 1980's Kathleen had founded The People for the Nipomo National Seashore (PNDNS) to work for the creation of a National Seashore in the dunes.

Soon after PNDNS began, an energetic young attorney named Elizabeth Scott-Graham was inspired to follow in Kathleen's footprints. Literally. Here was the ideal person to fathom murky bureaucratic channels. In her quest to present a case for the dunes to become a National Seashore, Liz found sympathy from California Senator Alan Cranston, but none from the area's member of the House of Representatives. Faced with the necessity to create a groundswell of opinion, she formed a speaker's bureau and seemed well on her way when a well-known Santa Maria businessman, George Smith, proposed a harbor at the mouth of the Santa Maria River.

Forced to divert her attention from acquisition to protecting the dunes from yet another incompatible development, Liz eventually defeated it and two other harbor proposals by simply presenting hard numbers to prove the fiscal impossibility of keeping sand from silting up such an anchorage.

Liz then learned of a proposed statewide bond issue that would provide half a billion dollars for parks and wildlife. She persuaded the organizers to include the dunes, and called upon the Sierra Club's muscle, as well as the Santa Lucia Chapter's dedicated members, to persuade the bond proponents to include funding for dunes acquisition; then, locally, her recruits spent a lot of time outside of grocery stores, gathering over 30,000 signatures.

When the issue passed with sixty-two percent voter approval, the dunes effort was granted $14 million. The funds were channeled through the Coastal Conservancy to the Nature Conservancy which actually carried out the willing seller acquisitions. Eventually the money secured the protection of Dune Lakes, Black

Lake, the 3,200 acre Mobile Coastal Preserve, Rancho Guadalupe
Dunes and part of the Point Sal area. There are still gaps along the
eighteen miles of dunes including privately owned land in the
LeRoy Trust and the Unocal Oil Field.

During the entire 1980's, Liz Scott-Graham had been working
pro bono. She left the area to work for a national nonprofit organization; in the meantime The Nature Conservancy set up temporary storefront quarters in 1996 as an Interpretative Center. In
December of 2000, with Kathleen present for the opening, the
Guadalupe Nipomo Dune Center moved to Craftsman house, a
restored building on the main street of Guadalupe. There adults as
well as children, can get a good overview and be introduced to
some of its inhabitants through interactive exhibits. Liz Scott-
Graham is Dunes Program Manager—heir to Kathleen's crusade.
Funded by grants and private donations, the Center established the
Kathleen Goddard Jones Endowment to honor Kathleen's long
commitment to the dunes. The income will be used to educate the
public and children about this marvelous and important habitat.

When fishermen and surfers complained about finding oil
near the mouth of the Santa Maria River, it was discovered that the
area was contaminated. For at least forty years Unocal had been
pumping about nine million gallons of diluent, a substance used to
thin the tar-like Santa Maria crude oil, into the Guadalupe Oil
Field. Beneath the dunes, the diluent gradually moved toward the
sea, resulting in what has been called one of the largest oil spills in
United States history. Unocal agreed to clean up the damage and
pay a $43.8 million fine. Kathleen was particularly shocked that
so many Unocal employees had known what was going on, and
continued the practice long after its negative impacts were well
established. The clean-up began in 1999 and is expected to take
four years.

Now vehicles are allowed on a very small portion of the dunes.
Some people advocate for their total removal; others are of the
opinion that it's better to sponsor an area where they can be closely supervised.

Gaylord died in 1991, just before his ninety-first birthday. Kathleen, a mere eighty-one, discovered that the pool of available suitors had just about dried up. But that didn't prevent her from keeping a sharp eye out for any younger prospect that might wander into her orbit.

With her own children scattered, the community itself became her extended family. Once in early winter of 1994 she lost her way on the dunes at night, in bad weather. Everybody who heard about it dropped what they were doing and joined in the search. A helicopter was called. She was rescued by a team of State Park Rangers and environmentalists that cut her out of a poison oak, blackberry and willow thicket—weak with hyperthermia and frightened by her brush with mortality—but game for the next hike.

When she was hit by a car on Thanksgiving eve in 1995—and barely survived—her phalanx of friends saw to it that she got on her feet again. She stubbornly refused to revisit the dunes until she could do so on her own two feet—leading a group. It took two years, but on New Years Day, 1998, she led a short hike onto the dunes in the annual celebration of the founding of the dune campaign, a ritual she had observed since 1962.

At age ninety-four Kathleen has lived to see her goal accomplished. Through a complicated set of territorial acquisitions the dunes are safe. She has been honored by many groups, from the Daughters of the American Revolution to the Sierra Club Oral History Project. Countless newspapers and magazines have featured her work. No longer do doubters sneer at "that crazy old lady who always shows up at meetings." Those who had underestimated her did so at their peril.

Other serious environmentalists who had helped her with the dunes would occasionally ask her to return the favor by getting involved in their pet causes. She would reply: "I'm sorry, but I must devote my efforts to the dunes."

Yet she was relieved when Lee Wilson, too, managed to win his long battle for Lopez Canyon. After lobbying, traveling to Washington, D.C., leading hikes and attending countless hearings, Wilson and Harold Miossi managed to get the Santa Lucia Wilderness—which includes Lopez—dedicated in 1978. With the dunes safe, Kathleen was inclined to overlook past quarrels, even the strident opposition and bullying ways of Lee Wilson; after all, no doubt he too had been operating under heavy emotional pressures.

Kathleen saw the need for a small book to be used by people who want to identify flora on the dunes. In the spring of 2001 *The Dune Mother's Wildflower Guide* was published under the auspices of the California Native Plant Society. Nineteen of Gaylord's photos were used, along with many by other photographers. Malcolm McLeod wrote the text with the assistance of Norm Hammond, E. Craig Cunningham, Jack and Grace Beigle. When its authors' placed the finished book into her hands she was overjoyed with the realization of yet another goal.

Many people helped Kathleen save the dunes, and she has been careful to give them great credit. But it was *her* obsession that impelled her to write thousands of letters, to learn the Latin names of every plant; it was *her* obsession that sent her to every city, county, regional, state or federal hearing that dealt with her dunes. Her attention never wandered to a different cause; she remained steadfast to her passion for over thirty years.

Although robbed by time of most of her hearing, she continued to attend meetings. Her mere presence added authority to any cause. People vied to greet her as an old friend or to meet her so they could claim acquaintance.

In her later years she joined the Bahá'i faith. Devoutly convinced that the future will belong to the inclusive teachings of its prophet, Bahá'u'lláh, she nevertheless likes to visit a local Christian church on a rousing Sunday like Easter when the music will be particularly moving—and loud.

On clear days, motorists traveling south on U.S. 101 can look beyond the town of Pismo Beach to see a gleaming strand of yellow—sometimes a thin sweep of beachfront; occasionally a vast swoop of dunes. Those who take the trouble to get out of their cars to explore this unique landscape can thank Kathleen Goddard Jones—who cared more for those who will come after her than she ever did for herself.

ABOUT THE AUTHOR

When Virginia Cornell wrote *Doc Susie: The True Story of a Country Physician in the Colorado Rockies*, she discovered a rich vein of American lore just waiting to be mined. Cornell's varied background—she has been a college teacher, ski lodge operator, mother, small-town weekly newspaper owner, art historian, lecturer, editor and publisher—provides a panoramic background for from which to draw. The research skills she gained in pursuit of her Ph.D. from Arizona State University equipped her to delve into the lives of notable women. With her sculptor-husband Don Longmire she lives on a California avocado ranch—along with a large dog and two cats. Various cruise lines have invited her to lecture on subjects ranging from art to literature to geology. A renaissance woman herself, she is dedicated to rescuing the stories of women of substance from oblivion.

Doc Susie: The True Story of a Country Physician in the Colorado Rockies by Virginia Cornell

She was beautiful, She was smart, She was dying . . . but when Susan Anderson, M.D., learned how badly mountain people needed her, she hurried to save the lives of her patients: On trains, On snowshoes, On horseback, On sleighs, On foot. Her only protector was the trusty .38 in her medical bag.

Ski Lodge: Adventures in Snow Business — by Virginia Cornell

High in the mountains, there was once a rustic, homemade ski lodge—populated by reluctant honeymooners, errant husbands, truant plumbers, youthful ski bums . . . plus one naive innkeeper.

The Latest Wrinkle and Other Signs of Aging — by Virginia Cornell

She laughs in the face of aging! Is there anything funny about fractured families, curmudgeonly husbands, family reunions, pets that kill, obituaries, gum disease, burial plans and Chia Pets? In Cornelll's hands there definitely is.

Maverick Women: Nineteenth Century Women Who Kicked Over the Traces by Frances Laurence

They were scholars, They were saints, They were sinners . . . They were determined. In a time when a woman's mind was kept as tightly laced as her corset, these females went against family, friends and convention to glaze trails for their sisters to come.

Around the World in 80 Years: Newsrooms, Sound Stages, Private Encounters and Public Affairs — by Ted Berkman

This is the story of a globe-trotting gadfly who, bent on winnowing truth from self-serving hokum, pursued a maverick path between Hong Kong and Hollywood, Cairo and Seville. It is simultaneously an intimate personal history and a wide-ranging saga of media creativity.

Plus, new editions of best-selling books by Ted Berkman: *Cast A Giant Shadow: The Story of Mickey Marcus Who Died to Save Jerusalem; Sabra: The Story of the Men and Women Behind the Guns of Israel; The Lady and The Law: The Remarkable Story of Fanny Holtzmann; To Seize The Passing Dream: A Novel of Whistler, His Women and His World*

For more information about these and other books from MANIFEST PUBLICATIONS, visit our website:

www.manifestpub.com

MANIFEST PUBLICATIONS ORDER FORM

www.manifestpub.com

Fax orders with your Purchase Order number to 805.684.3100.
If you have questions, please call 805.684.4905 or email
vcornell@manifestpub.com.
Or you may mail your order to:
Manifest Publications, P.O. Box 429 Carpinteria, CA 93014-0429

I wish to order:

___ tradepaper copies of <u>Defender of the Dunes</u>/$14.95 ea.   _____

___ tradepaper copies of <u>Doc Susie</u>/$14.95 ea.   _____

___ tradepaper copies of <u>Ski Lodge</u>/$12.95 ea.   _____

___ tradepaper copies of <u>The Latest Wrinkle</u>/$9.95 ea   _____

___ tradepaper copies of <u>Maverick Women</u>/$18.50 ea   _____

___ hardbound copies of <u>Around the World in 80 Years</u>/$19.95 ea.   _____

+ Shipping: Priority Mail, $5 per order   _____

+ Sales Tax, 7.75% (California only)   _____

TOTAL PURCHASE   _____

Send order to:

Name _____

Street Address/P.O. Box _____

_____

City _____

State _____ Zip _____

Daytime Phone Number_____

Email Address_____